■ THE CASTING HANDBOOK

FOR FILM AND THEATRE MAKERS

Casting is a crucial creative element of any production – and yet the craft and skills needed to put together a successful and exciting cast are often overlooked. *The Casting Handbook* explains the casting process from beginning to end and covers everything producers and directors need to know – as well as proving a fascinating and illuminating read for actors. The book explores:

- how to prepare a breakdown
- where to source actors
- how to prepare for a casting session
- how to make casting decisions
- how a cast is put together
- how deals are done
- ethics and the law, with special reference to casting children
- how casting decisions are made, from fringe theatre to Hollywood blockbusters.

The Casting Handbook considers actors', producers', agents' and directors' relationships with a casting director; the day-to-day work that is casting; and how a professional and informed approach can make a huge difference to the final product.

Including interviews with actors, agents, directors, casting directors and producers; case studies; exercises; and a fact file of useful templates and contacts, this book offers a thorough induction into the casting process, suitable for students and early career professionals in any media.

Suzy Catliff assisted and directed in regional repertory theatres, before becoming casting assistant on *Sense and Sensibility*, *The English Patient* and *Wilde* as well as numerous other films, television series and dramas. Suzy was casting director for BBC1's flagship drama *Casualty* for three years amongst other TV and film projects, including the award-winning *D-Day*, *Silent Witness*, *Sir Gadabout* and UK casting on two series of *Primeval* for ITV. She is currently UK casting consultant for Shaftesbury Films. Suzy also works in drama schools, universities and film schools as a director, casting director and teacher.

Jennifer Granville has worked as an actor in repertory and West End theatre, film and TV. Her screenplays have won the La Femme, 21st Century and Latino screenwriting competitions. Producing credits include: *The Secret Songs of Butterfish*, which won the Gold Plaque, Chicago International Film Festival and Special Jury Award at the New York Expo; *On the Roof*, a Fuji Award-winning short; *The Real Fawlty Towers*, for Anglia Television directed by Lindy Heymann; and the experimental *Winesburg, Ohio* adapted from the Sherwood Anderson book of the same name. Her experimental screenplay *MSI: The Anatomy of Integers and Permutations* is currently being adapted into a graphic novel by Princeton University Press. She taught at the Ohio University School of Film in the USA and since 2005 has been Director of the Northern Film School at Leeds Metropolitan University.

The Casting Handbook

for Film and Theatre Makers

By Suzy Catliff and Jennifer Granville

Routledge
Taylor & Francis Group

LONDON AND NEW YORK

First published 2013
by Routledge
2 Park Square, Milton Park, Abingdon, Oxon OX14 4RN

Simultaneously published in the USA and Canada
by Routledge
711 Third Avenue, New York, NY 10017

Routledge is an imprint of the Taylor & Francis Group, an
informa business

British Library Cataloguing in Publication Data
A catalogue record for this book is available from the
British Library

Library of Congress Cataloging in Publication Data
Catliff, Suzy.
The casting handbook : for film and theatre makers /
Suzy Catliff, Jennifer Granville.
p. cm.
Includes bibliographical references and index.
1. Motion pictures--Casting. 2. Theater--Casting. I.
Granville, Jennifer. II. Title.
PN1995.9.C34C38 2013
791.4302'8--dc23
2012029346

ISBN: 978-0-415-68822-2(hbk)
ISBN: 978-0-415-68824-6(pbk)
ISBN: 978-0-203-14341-4(ebk)

Typeset in Helvetica
by Saxon Graphics Ltd, Derby DE21 4SZ

MIX
Paper from
responsible sources
FSC® C004839
www.fsc.org

Printed and bound in Great Britain by
TJ International Ltd, Padstow, Cornwall

■ CONTENTS

■ EXERCISES, CHECKLISTS AND EXAMPLES

■ ACKNOWLEDGEMENTS

Thank you to Miriam Manley for her thorough, insightful and brutally honest reading of the first unwieldy draft and thank you to Leo Kirby for continuing in the same vein! Thanks also to Isabelle Amyes, Tim Bradley, David Danislovsky, Guy Farrar, Sue Golay, Akbar Kurtha and Ann Tobin for reading and giving such useful feedback. Thank you to Roy Chandler for allowing us to use Fleur's Spotlight CV, to Stuart Bunce and Bryony Afferson – both with Jeremy Brook Ltd, and to Georgina Landau for allowing us to print their CVs. Thank you to everybody who gave so generously of their time, knowledge and experience in the contributing interviews. Thank you to all the students we have worked with and learned from, and to our colleagues who have supported and encouraged us during the writing of this book. Finally thanks to all the fantastic people at Routledge who guided us through the very steep learning curve of publishing - Aileen Storry, Eileen Strebernik. Natalie Foster, Stacy Carter, Lorna Hawes and the endlessly patient and meticulous Rob Brown at Saxon Graphics.

We dedicate this book to all the actors who regularly put themselves on the front line – giving their talent and experience purely in pursuit of making great work.

■ INTRODUCTION

*It's hugely important. Hugely important. Without a decent cast,
you're sunk*

Megan Wheldon – agent

The Casting Handbook is a practical, easy-to-use tool for anyone
who is intending to ask actors to take part in their production. The
book describes the process of casting in theatre, film, television
and radio: leading you through the practicalities of how to do it
professionally and efficiently – from having your script prepared
and ready, to the first day of rehearsals or principle photography.

The book is a guide for early career producers and directors and
will remain a useful reference throughout your career. It is also a
vital teaching tool for drama schools, film schools, colleges and
universities.

We believe that directors and producers, and their teams, should
be just as well prepared in how to cast as the actor should be in
how to audition. Whilst audition technique is part of an actor's
toolkit, and there are many 'how to' books that cover it in detail,
casting technique has not been given the same level of attention.

The Casting Handbook will also be an enlightening read for actors,
giving much needed perspective. When an actor doesn't get a role,
they very often think it is because they messed up, that they didn't
try hard enough, didn't look right or just weren't good enough.
Actors reading this book will understand how many factors are
involved in any casting decision, giving them insight into what
happens on the other side of the desk.

Casting is a creative process. Like all creative processes it requires
skill, practice and confidence. We offer you methods and advice
that, together with your own creativity and personal taste, will

help you find that unique chemistry that brings a script to life and delivers your vision.

A fantastic range of industry professionals have generously shared their experience, opinions and advice with us. What they all have in common is a respect for actors, a knowledge of casting and an understanding of its importance and power.

Suzy Catliff and Jennifer Granville

Casting is one of the fundamental planks when you are thinking conceptually about the project. Well before you have got a script, you need to think about how you are going to cast.

Marc Samuelson – producer

■ HOW TO USE THIS BOOK

CHAPTERS

The Casting Handbook takes you through the process of casting chronologically. The Chapters are clearly labelled, so it is easy to reference the process you are looking for. Chapters can be used independently if you need guidance in a specific area – for example 'Chapter 10 – Casting Children'.

There are exercises to help you practice the methods we talk about, and there are charts and templates to help you get organized in planning and administering the casting for your production.

CASE STUDIES

In between each of the chapters there is an interview we conducted with professional producers, directors, casting directors, agents and actors. All of them are connected and crucial to the casting process. Each case study expands on topics covered within the *The Casting Handbook* chapters.

We focus on the process for theatre and film casting, rather than for television, because it is unlikely you would cast for television without some experience of either of the other two mediums. We use the experience of the many television professionals interviewed for the book, to advise and comment on TV casting.

PROFESSIONAL PRACTITIONERS

Throughout the book we use quotes from our professional practitioners, which give excellent advice on how to cast, along with reflections on the nature of casting. Our practitioners range from Oscar-winning directors and producers to jobbing actors. At the back of the book you will find short biographies of them all, giving a context for their contributions.

GLOSSARY

In all chapters there are words used that may need clarification. These are highlighted where they occur, and defined in the margin of that page. You can also turn to the Glossary at the back of the book.

APPENDICES

Listings of organizations, useful websites, templates for charts and forms used in the book, exercises and scripts can all be found in the appendices.

LEGAL

We advocate that you make yourself aware of the legal requirements in pay, insurance, volunteering, licensing and health and safety. *The Casting Handbook* can advise where legal requirements need to be considered, but cannot detail the requirements themselves, as legislation is constantly changing. It is essential to ensure that you are adhering to the most up-to-date legislation in all areas.

■ WHAT IS CASTING?

It's the best bit!

Jo Ward – producer

What do you think about when you remember your favourite film? Why do you enjoy a particular television programme? When you come out of the theatre enraptured by what you have seen – what made it so exciting? It may be the set, the lighting, the locations, the camera angles or the dialogue but it is bound to include the characters that have been created and how they told the story.

You can't get a character – and the actor – out of your head. Not necessarily a star, not necessarily the lead role, not necessarily anyone you have ever seen before, but someone whose honesty and truth shines through, someone who touches you, moves you and stays with you.

Where do these artists come from? How do they end up on your stage or screen, breathing life into the words and making the characters totally believable?

Casting is the key.

DEFINITIONS OF CASTING

☐ *The form or appearance of something, especially someone's features.'*

Oxford English Dictionary

When you read a script, you are bound to imagine what the characters look like.

☐ *The overall appearance of someone's skin or hair as determined by a tinge of a particular colour*

Oxford English Dictionary

Casting is not about finding a particular hair or skin colour. In the script of 'Some Like it Hot' Billy Wilder describes Sugar as "the dream girl of every red blooded American male." He does not describe her hair and skin colour.

☐ *The character of something*

Oxford English Dictionary

Casting is about defining the character to tell the story. For example, Steve Martin played a modern day Cyrano in the film Roxanne. He didn't have the vital physical attribute of a big nose; what he did have was the character, wit and charisma that was vital for the role.

☐ *Be cast in a mould (of the person) be of the type specified*

Oxford English Dictionary

To cast an actor to type, means to cast them in a type of role that they are known for playing. For example, Tom Cruise is famous for playing action heroes.

☐ *Cast one's eyes over – have a quick appraising look at*

Oxford English Dictionary

Casting is rarely quick.

☐ *Cast about (or around or round) – search far and wide (physically or mentally) – go in all directions*

Oxford English Dictionary

Casting is all about researching, and searching, to find the right actor for the part.

A BRIEF HISTORY OF CASTING

Casting is the essence. It's where you start and where you finish. Because if you get the casting right you've got the heart and soul of the production right

Marina Caldarone – director

Casting has been around for as long as there have been productions to cast. Whether or not the early producers picked from two people they knew, or rang up a friend to see if they were free, the process of casting was underway. From the Greeks to the Mystery Plays to radio and the Lumiere Brothers, there was a decision about who was going to play what. And that is casting.

Repertory
A permanent company that produces regular work.

Types
For example, leading man, ingénue, character actor, leading lady, juvenile lead.

THEATRE

In the 1930s, when weekly **repertory** theatres were established in many regions of the UK, the theatre manager would often engage a company of actors, from a range of **types** to serve the many different plays. The actors would learn a new part every week and remain at the theatre for a season. That gradually changed, as rehearsal times lengthened and plays ran for longer periods, leading up to the present day where plays in repertory theatre are usually cast individually.

In West End theatre, the focus has always been on casting **star** names to attract audiences and revenue. In the early twentieth century, the casting was carried out by a combination of writer, director and producer. Only in the last 20 years, have casting directors become more common.

Star
An actor whose name is instantly recognizable to audiences.

FILM

All the early Ealing comedies, the Ranks – war time films and so on – they always had a casting director-
                    Robert Banks Stewart – producer/writer

From the mid-1920s the casting was undertaken by casting directors working out of the various studios situated around London; Pinewood, Elstree, Ealing, Shepperton and Twickenham. From the early 1960s, freelance casting directors also worked for the studios, without being based there. Casting director Miriam Brickman, for example, began working at the Royal Court Theatre, then went on to cast films including Lindsay Anderson's *If*. She had offices in Half Moon Street and her assistants included the next generation of casting directors such as Mary Selway, Joyce Nettles and Susie Figgis.

The early casting directors for film were responsible for finding the actors and overseeing the administration and organization necessary. A studio would normally have one casting director and an assistant, who would be on the permanent staff and required to be members of the **ACTT** trade union. They would look after their studio's needs and requirements.

ACTT
The Association of Cinematographers and Allied Technicians merged with the Broadcasting and Entertainment Trades Alliance forming the Broadcasting, Entertainment, Cinematograph and Theatre Union – BECTU – in 1991.

TELEVISION

There was a strict division between BBC and ITV – Dangerman, Interpol Calling – these were done as mini-films, and because they were being made in film studios there was normally a casting director. Somebody else did the contracts – called 'Artists' Contracts' at the BBC.
                    Robert Banks Stewart – producer/writer

With the advent of television, casting was undertaken by the producer and director with secretaries to assist. Gradually, as television drama expanded and more actors were needed, casting directors were employed by the major independent television companies. For example, Granada TV employed Doreen Jones and Malcolm Drury (who went on to be Head of Casting at Yorkshire TV), at Thames TV Pat O'Connell worked with Maggie Cartier, whilst Tony Arnell cast for ATV. They formed casting departments who were specifically employed to source actors.

There was a big difference between the BBC and the ITV companies in that casting directors weren't recognised as such by the BBC. They were known as 'casting advisers' up until the late 1990s because, the BBC argued, they did not negotiate the contracts. Many of these casting advisers, such as Sarah Bird and Angela Grosvenor, have gone on to make successful careers as freelance casting directors, very often casting major productions for the BBC.

Since 2000 there has been a casting department at the BBC which is responsible for a range of programmes including continuing dramas such as *EastEnders*, *Casualty*, *Holby City* and *Doctors*.

> *The whole point of having a casting department at Granada was that we were to go out and find people who were very good – but were cheap – to play the leads.*
>
> Doreen Jones – casting director

THE CASTING DIRECTORS GUILD

In 1997 Doreen Jones and Simone Reynolds met and talked about the possibility of a Guild. They were particularly anxious to address the problem of 'bad practice' by some casting directors (for example, the non-use of Equity agreements, actors being exploited, casting directors deliberately under-cutting each other, and various other problems which had come about since Margaret Thatcher had disbanded the unions – including the ACTT). This coincided with the Lottery being launched, and large sums of money being awarded to all kinds of individuals and companies, some of whom were simply using the funds to make 'tax break' films for both TV and the cinema. Many of these films never saw the light of day, or went straight to video. The problem of casting directors obtaining a proper credit on screen was rife and the BBC only reluctantly agreed to a credit of 'Casting Adviser'. Casting directors, like Lynn Stalmaster, in the USA were getting single screen credits whilst Mary Selway (a top UK casting director) was struggling to get a credit at all. Hence the Guild was set up in 1997, after a year of planning and consultation undertaken by the original committee, with Simone Reynolds as Chair. The other members of the committee were Anne Henderson, Doreen Jones, Julia Duff, Audrey Helps and Paul De Freitas.

Case Study – the first time film director

J Blakeson was a jobbing screenwriter looking for an opportunity to direct a feature. His agent liked a thriller he had written (as a sample for a potential writing gig) and sent it out on the understanding that J would only sell it if someone let him direct it – which Cinema NX finally did.

JB: I wanted to write something that I could do on my own so I wrote a film called *The Disappearance of Alice Creed*. As a writer trying to get something made to direct myself, I wrote it with actors that I knew I could probably get to do it on favours. I knew more male actors than female actors, so I wrote it for two men and a woman.

Q: And then it got financed?

JB: Yes, and we had what was called 'a cast dependent green light', which means that they say they are going to make the movie but only if they have the right cast. They use this phrase 'Do they mean something?' And it's a very fluid thing because they do comparisons on actors: What's this actor been in before? In a similar role? How much money did that make? What does an actor mean to a sales agent? Can they sell that to different territories around the world?

So I wrote my list of every actor I could think of for each role. The producers wrote their list and then we combined lists. And we hired a fantastic casting director – Lucy Bevan.

Q: As a writer/director did you have a clear picture in your head of your characters?

JB: Yes, and that had a big effect in casting – I had to re-imagine the character of Vic for Eddie (Marsan). Eddie wasn't what was on the page: physically he was a much bigger, tougher character.

Q: So did you have to change the script for him?

JB: No, I just had to change the way I thought about the script. I was very resistant to Eddie when the producers suggested him. They'd worked with him before and he meant something – and he's a great actor. I just couldn't equate him with the character. We were seeing lots of other people and then I thought 'What am I doing? I'm chasing these people because they look right and they aren't as good as Eddie. I'm being an idiot.'

Q: So, how was working with an actor who was so experienced?

JB: He came very prepared. We talked about the character and Eddie had an absolute idea of what he wanted to do, but we were both making the same film. We wanted to get the same thing.

Q: And how did you describe the character of Alice to Lucy?

JB: Well, with the Alice character she can't be the victim, she can't be this screaming typical victim, she has to have something about her. She has to have this toughness and this fight back spirit and something behind her eyes. You have to believe she's scared but, once she's had enough, you have to believe that she can take control. So she's got this toughness to her.

Q: How did you arrive at Gemma Arterton?

JB: Lucy knew her work from the time she was at drama school, RADA, and the producers were very keen on her. I said I would consider her if she would come and read for us. She'd just finished the Prince of Persia the week before! It was all about the script. Gemma read it, liked it and really wanted to do it. So she came in and within about two seconds it was clear – even before she auditioned – it was clear just meeting her and talking to her.

Q: What about the Danny character – was it less clear who you would cast for that?

JB: Yeah – we saw a lot of people for Danny.

Q: Why did you see a lot? What were you looking for?

JB: Well, Danny was sort of from the wrong side of the tracks and he had to be very seductive and attractive and have an element of danger to him. Danny is the last person we cast and he's in 90 per cent of the film.

Q: How did you end up with Martin Compston?

JB: It was one of those weird things – we were ten days away from production – we'd built the sets but we didn't have our Danny. We were getting kind of desperate. There were a few actors on the table, but there were reservations in the room about whether they would work properly, especially as with a first time director there's a real risk that we were so desperate to get the film made, by any means necessary, that you'd cast anybody, and that's a mistake.

And one of the problems with casting Danny was that we had already cast Alice and Vic, and because there's three of them, and Danny has to have a very specific relationship with both of them, they all had to work together perfectly. Finding somebody to hit that was very hard, even just physically, because Eddie is not the tallest man in the world so casting someone who was six and a half foot would just look funny.

And, I think on the same day, all of us thought of Martin. I remembered seeing him in *Sweet Sixteen* and Andrea Arnold's film *Red Road*. And there's a moment in that when he gets Kate Dickie's character to go to look out of a window – and you really think he's going to push her out. He's this little cherubic-faced guy and its really tense, she opens this window, a gust of wind comes through the window, and it's sort of this utopian moment as she looks at him, and he's smiling and all of sudden it's like 'he is a nice guy!'– but, later on, he proves not to be a nice guy. So we asked him to put himself on tape – and he was good, really good.

Q: Did he read from the script?

JB: We sent sides, and there was somebody off camera doing the other part. But he had it – he'd learned it – that was quite impressive as he had quite a lot to say. So we asked him to come down and read with Gemma to see if the two of them would work together well; we were already rehearsing by this time. And Gemma and he did work well together. And, luckily, Martin was shorter than Eddie so that worked out very well too. You absolutely have to balance the actors against each other; it has to work out.

CHAPTER 1

WHERE TO START?

■ Arrange a reading
■ Research
■ Finding actors
■ Budget
☐ Case study – the actor

■ WHERE TO START?

Scripts and story have to come first, because without that you don't really have anything

Jason O'Mara – actor

You have been planning your production, your script is locked and you are ready to start casting. Whether you are working in film or theatre, you need to be sure that the script, and your vision for it, is as clear and as polished as it can possibly be.

You also need to be clear on your budget and the implications that this will have on how you go about finding and engaging the right actors for your project.

ARRANGE A READING:

A reading does exactly what it says on the tin. A group of people, each with a copy of the script, are assigned roles and read the script out loud. In the industry this is for the producer, writer and director to hear the script and sometimes sales agents, distributors, producers, artists' **agents** and other potentially interested parties are invited.

Agent
The actor's representative.

For any project, the creative team need to hear the script out loud, so you should get other people who are not working on the production to read it for you. Try and get actors to do it or, failing that, friends or relatives.

What you need at this stage is to hear it, to be the audience, to close your eyes and see the action, so you can react honestly and make notes – without worrying about reading lines.

You will be surprised at how different it sounds and feels when you actually *hear* it. And what great ideas you will get. The people reading it will view it from their character's perspective and they will tell you whether the dialogue trips easily off the tongue and if they feel that the character has a credible and satisfying emotional journey.

Hearing dialogue spoken, testing the dynamics between characters, discovering if the story makes sense and gauging a sense of the audience reaction are all benefits gained from a reading.

- Focus on finding good readers.
- Remember to ask someone to read the stage directions or **action**.
- Be ready to make notes and/or record the reading.
- Allow time at the end of the reading for discussion.

Action
The descriptions or stage directions in a script, i.e. not dialogue

New writing

If your script is new writing – that is, has never been performed in this version before – then you need to know that it works.

Previously produced work

If your project has already been produced a reading might not be as vital. However, if you have adapted a work – for example Romeo and Juliet for four actors – then it is advisable to read it before you move into casting and production.

> *It always comes back to the script! Casting has got to be a reflection of what is in the script.*
>
> Robert Banks Stewart – producer/writer

RESEARCH

> *There's an intelligence involved in casting, which means having a real knowledge about the piece and the characters, having real insight into the period, the class and the background of that character.*
>
> Jeremy Brook – agent

To cast intelligently, you need an understanding of the world that the character inhabits. Each project will have its own particular demands and requirements. Here are some common areas for research:

The world of the script

You need to get a feel for faces and body type, how people move, talk, dress and communicate in the time your production is set. All these elements are clear indicators of what actors will need to bring to the production.

- If you listen to British radio and television broadcasters from 50 years ago, it almost sounds as though it is another language. Therefore, if your production is set in the 1950s, you need to familiarize yourself with the authentic sound and accents of the period – of course, you may choose not to reproduce them exactly but, in order to make that choice, you need to have an informed point of reference.

■   Read contemporary books, fashion magazines, newspapers and adverts; watch and listen to radio, films and TV made in the period; and see plays written in the period.

■   Your script might require a character to speak in a particular language or accent, have a disability, or a specialized skill – such as tightrope walking. Now is the time to focus on the detail of what you will be requiring from your actors.

Research is a big part of all the other work you do before you get into the rehearsal room.'

Hannah Miller – head of casting, RSC

ACTORS

You need to become familiar with actors and their work, both on stage and on screen.

■   To do this successfully you need to see actors acting as frequently as possible.

You no doubt will already have your own taste and favourite actors. By watching actors, and analysing your reactions to their performance, you will develop your ability to analyse what it is you like and dislike about an actor and make informed decisions that will best serve your production.

Whatever the medium you are working in, don't limit yourself to only watching actors on TV or film – make the time to go and see a play in a theatre. It doesn't have to cost a fortune. You will see a greater diversity of the different scales, styles and range actors can achieve if you see them working in large theatres, fringe theatres and alternative spaces.

The most important thing is to steep yourselves in the business; go to the theatre, go to fringe plays, go to the cinema regularly. You must be interested, you must see people, be really enthusiastic about it - not just standing on the sidelines

Robert Banks Stewart – producer/writer

☐ Find out about the pool of actors available to you

This may be determined by location, budget or specific requirements of a script. For example, Jenny was supervising a student production which was written as a silent film that required three mime artists as the lead characters, so the advice given to the team was to find mime schools, groups, physical theatre companies and dance companies.

☐ Contact and build relationships with appropriate groups

This could mean local or specialist, depending on your requirements. For example, find your local clubs or community centres for different nationalities. See if they have a drama club, find out when they meet and go along to their workshops.

Try and find a way to experience the world of your character, so that you will be able to cast authentically.

☐ Where an actor is based is a vital consideration

Can you afford to pay for accommodation and travel? You may decide you can afford to pay for several actors from outside your area – or you may decide that everyone has to be within walking distance of rehearsals or your location.

Once you know what you can afford, you can focus your research, which means finding out about:

- regional and local theatres
- film networks
- drama schools
- performing arts/theatre/drama university courses
- local branches of Equity.

Find out what TV is made in your area. It is particularly worth watching local television drama as there might be an actor playing a regular character who is on the lookout for an interesting project that they could fit into their schedules.

BUDGET

In an ideal world you would employ your actors on a standard industry contract and pay them accordingly. You should always consult the **appropriate industry organization** to find out the latest guidelines and advice.

Appropriate industry organization
See details under 'Trade & Industry organizations' in the Appendices.

Here are the budgetary items you need to think about:

■   Actors' Fees – Refer to the appropriate guidelines provided by the relevant organization or union. This may mean setting aside an amount for fees. Whether or not you are involved in a student production, you will be aiming to engage professional actors and so, at the very least, you will be covering their **expenses.** Although you may only be able to pay your actors expenses, that doesn't mean you can't approach an experienced actor.

Expenses
Costs incurred by the actor in order to work on a project.

■   Accommodation – An actor will expect the production to pay for any accommodation if they are away from their home base.

■   Travel Costs – You should not expect an actor to pay for buses, taxis, petrol or air fare to get to the place where they are working. They will need all travel costs reimbursed.

■   Subsistence – If the actor is away from their home base, you will need to ensure that they will have either a per diem allowance or food provided.

■   Make-up – Don't expect actors to provide their own make-up. Some will, but it is still an item to have in your budget.

■   Costume – You must budget for costume or for cleaning and/ or damage if you are going to ask actors to wear their own clothes.

■   Copies of the film – If it is a film project, you *must* deliver a copy of the film to the actor and their agent (or as many copies as they would like). Assuming they are not paid, this is the only reward the actor is getting for being in your film – they will be able to use clips for their show reel.

■   Casting director – This is not a necessity but is a potential cost. If you are thinking of approaching a casting director, watch their work. Identify what it is about their work that makes you want to collaborate with them. For more information on casting directors, please read Chapter 4.

☐   Finding a common language with your team

By finding a common language you can make sure that you are all searching for the same thing. When you are thinking about the actors, think about the story you are telling; and the atmosphere and feeling you want to create. Ensure that you allow just as much time for the process of casting as for budgeting and scheduling.

You might have been thinking about casting from the moment you started work on the script. But, unless you are collaborating with an artist and specifically developing a script for them, you won't know who is going to play what role.

One of my mates is Ray Winstone and if he says to me "why don't you write this for me", then I'll think about it, but generally I'll try and write something for the character – I don't want to think about who it might be because usually, the minute I do that, the actor turns it down and I'm really disappointed

Simon Mirren – writer/producer

QUALITIES

One of the reasons why a **star** is cast in a production – whether it is stage, screen, radio or animation – is because that particular star brings qualities to the role that are unique. When *you* think of a star you will not just think of them in physical terms like 'blonde', 'muscular', 'fit' or 'tall', but you will also think of them as 'quirky', 'sensuous', 'sinister' or 'dangerous'.

Star
An actor whose name is instantly recognizable to an audience.

Every human being has their own distinguishing qualities which are not dependant on, or defined by, their physicality. For instance, you may describe a character as generous and open or conversely as mean or cold.

However your response to actors can be quite different to that of your collaborators. You need to understand your taste *and* their taste. For example, you might not agree with the qualities we have given Tom Cruise below, but if you were about to cast him in a film, you and your team would need to have decided what qualities you were looking for and whether Tom Cruise fitted the bill.

☐ Try doing the following exercises.

In the chart below we name six actors and identify qualities that we think define them.

ACTOR	QUALITIES
Emily Blunt	Warmth, humour, empathy
Michael Fassbender	Energy, intensity
Michelle Williams	Sexuality, vulnerability
Hugh Jackman	Physicality, humour
Gary Oldman	Dangerous, versatile
Halle Berry	Sexuality, fragility

■ **Exercise 1**

Using this same list of qualities, each member of your creative
team should independently name other actors that they think have
them.

QUALITIES	ACTOR
Warmth, humour, empathy	
Energy, intensity	
Sexuality, vulnerability	
Physicality, cheekiness	
Warmth, intelligence	
Sexuality, humour	

Now, compare notes with your collaborators. You may be
surprised how differently you define these qualities.

■ **Exercise 2**

This exercise will help articulate your taste.

FAVOURITE ACTORS	REASONS

FAVOURITE ACTRESSES	REASONS

■ **Exercise 3**

Choose your favourite actor or actress from different genres. This exercise will help you identify the qualities actors can bring to enrich a production.

GENRE	ACTOR	REASONS
Action		
Costume/historical		
Fantasy		
Animation		
Thriller		
Musical		
Zombie		
Horror		

To help you identify the qualities different actors can bring to a theatre production, name your favourite actor or actress who you have seen perform in the following.

GENRE	ACTOR	REASONS
Classical		
New writing		
Comedy		
Contemporary		
Shakespeare		
Musical		
Site Specific		
Pantomime		
Stand up		

■ Exercise 4 – knowing your taste

This exercise is to help you to think about your taste and to articulate it.

Think of six actors: three women and three men, with an assortment of ages and nationalities.

What is it you like about them? What qualities do they have?

GENDER	AGE	NATIONALITY	ACTOR	WHAT DO YOU LIKE ABOUT THEM	DEFINING QUALITIES
Male	17 – 25	British			
Female	17 – 25	British			
Male	60+	North American			
Female	60+	North American			
Male	35 – 40	European			
Female	35 – 40	European			

This is completely subjective – remember it is *your* voice and *your* opinion that you are defining.

It is surprisingly hard to really nail it first go but, luckily, it is a skill that you can practice every time you watch a performance and think about the actors and their qualities

Now it is time for you and your team to look at your own script.

Each member of your team should do their own chart. Write down the principal characters you are looking for.

Put in your dream team casting… imagine the biggest budget and the whole galaxy of acting talent… who would you cast and, most importantly, why?

CHARACTER	GENDER	AGE	NATIONALITY/ETHNICITY	ACTOR	WHAT DO YOU LIKE ABOUT THEM	DEFINING QUALITIES

Now compare notes and if you differ wildly in your ideas, talk about why. Discuss how it would affect the dynamic of your story if you were to cast one actor instead of another.

Case Study – the actor

Jason O'Mara *started his career in Ireland and, via regional repertory theatre and several popular TV series, made his way to Hollywood, USA, where he is now able to pick and choose his work.*

Q: What about young filmmakers who feel you are the right person for their scripts? Do you ever consider them?

JOM: I have received scripts like that in the past and have definitely considered doing them – they should really come through the agent you know? Otherwise it's very hard for the actor to go 'Listen this guy rang me up and gave me this script and they are shooting this weekend and I think I'm going to go and do it' and the agent's like 'Wait, wait, wait a second! What script? What is this? Who is making this?' Because you have to convince the agent to do something for no money. You're also not going to want to give up a week or two of your life, not seeing your kids, or not being at home and going off to whatever wild and windy location they want you to go off to – unless the script is great.

Young filmmakers have to remember – it's not just if the script is better than the student next to you, or if it's the best script of the year – if you want good actors you're competing on a really high level because good actors read good scripts all the time. So, if you want to get good actors first of all the script needs to be good, the story needs to be good, it needs to be a good character but also that actor is going to want be able to say 'I'm proud of this work I've done' and not just that the director made something really 'arty'.

Here's the thing I learned: when I went to Hollywood, working on a TV series, the first few months I was there, I got this idea for an episode. I just thought it was the best idea ever and I called the producer and show runner, Sean Cassidy, and said 'I've got this great idea for an episode' and he said 'Have you written a script?' and I said 'No, it's an idea, I haven't written it yet!' and he goes 'Well call me when you've written the script. Ideas are two-a-penny in Hollywood. Come to me with a script and if you work through it thoroughly, have crafted the story and everything works, and you have A B C D stories, and they all intersect, and it delivers with a punch at the end, and involves every character that we have on set here that's available – then I will consider it!' Suddenly that was a very different proposition.

Ideas are two-a-penny – that's the first rule and the second rule is – scripts aren't worth anything unless they have been honed, crafted and re-worked. Anyone can sit and write a script in a day, or two days.

I know because I have written a lot of crap scripts. Really crap. That's the other thing... students (and I say this because I was a student once, a long time ago). Students can be so critical of Hollywood and studios, and while it should be criticized (and who better to do it than the next generation) there is a lot to be said for it. I've come to a new appreciation for it: a lot of work goes into it and nobody, not even Hollywood writers or directors, want to make a bad film, nobody ever wants to make a bad film.

Q: Do you think casting is creative?

JOM: It has to be creative – it's a huge undertaking and there has to be a lot of creativity involved. You know, they've got a filmmaker saying 'I want this type for this' and they usually name an actor like 'I want a Michael Caine type' or ' an Angelina Jolie type' for this role, but they don't actually want Michael Caine or Angelina Jolie because they don't have the money. So they want that kind of person but between the ages of 25 and 34 and also they want them to be, you know, African or Irish.

So the casting director has to go through the Rolodex in their mind and figure out who they're going to bring in for this, but at the same time they have to be able to suggest other things: 'Well, what if he was Chinese and not Irish?'

I think it's amazing how the casting director matches this group of actors with this character, and that group of actors with that character and, at the same time, finds the only actor who can play that role. The really good casting director can find the perfect actor for that role, sometimes the only actor who could play that role. I just find that astounding.

Q: How much contact do you have on big projects (like Terra Nova) with the next layers up above the casting directors?

JOM: Oh well, it all depends on where you are in the pecking order. What kind of star you are. Sometimes you get to talk to the producer and director and they will woo you onto the project, and sometimes you're the one who is going to have to go into the room and fight for the role. I had a talent holding deal with ABC for five years, so sometimes I would get a pick of three different scripts for ABC and I would choose one, or the president of the network would call me and say 'Look, I know you like this one, but this is the one we would really like you to do'. That kind of conversation is at a very high level.

You start those conversations with Steve McPherson, who used to run ABC, and I would still have those sorts of conversations with Kevin Riley who runs FOX, because we wanted to do something together. Those are the kind of heights I didn't know existed for a long time until I had something to offer these places, then I started to have those kind of conversations. Obviously those kinds of conversations do exclude a casting director to a great extent.

So Kevin Riley and I wanted to do something together and Terra Nova came along... obviously Steven Spielberg had to sign off on me – I didn't go into the room to read for it, I submitted a showreel, some scenes. Steven Spielberg watched those and returned his verdict back to the network and the production company, DreamWorks, and they offered me the role. So that's how that happened. ...it's a different level to how I worked for 15 years; it was like a little secret door opened that I didn't know was there. Like 'Oh, you think this is the nice room? No, the nice room is in the back, come with us'.

And then you're in that room and you're like 'oh no, there's a nicer room than this...'

CHAPTER 2

THE BREAKDOWN

- ■ What is a breakdown?
- ■ Examples of breakdowns
- ■ What you need to put in your breakdown
- ☐ Case study – the agent

■ THE BREAKDOWN

They must catch the spirit.

Robert Banks Stewart – producer/writer

To find a cast you need to define what you are looking for and you need to get that information out to the appropriate people.

Communication is the key to a successful production and the breakdown is the first step. Initially, the point of writing a breakdown is to help you define and describe the characters in your production.

You need to write a clear and concise character breakdown for every speaking role in your script.

Below is an example of one of Suzy's casting breakdowns for a script from the television series *Silent Witness*. Through the process of writing this breakdown, Suzy was able to define the qualities of each character. You will see how clear her descriptions are, whilst leaving plenty of room for a wide and diverse variety of actors to be considered for each part.

Example of a character breakdown

Brenda – Early thirties

A single parent, attractive and sexy in a tarty sort of a way. Like her son, she's had her childhood taken from her by the poverty of her background. Like her friends, she got pregnant young and lives on benefits. She is a hopeless mum and although deep down she loves her kids and in a way does her best, she's simply not equipped for her life.

Detective Superintendent David Riley – Forties

Part of the Trident 'black-on-black crime unit' Riley has seen it all. When we first meet him we may think he's rather critical and even lazy; as the story progresses we will come to understand that he knows full well that he can only achieve a tiny amount of what needs to be done in this social stratum. World weary and an adherent of the realpolitik.

T-Boy Thomas – 20

The leading gangster in the area, T-Boy is all flash car and bling – modelled carefully on pop video rap stars. T-Boy has had an illustrious career and has killed a number of times – he's violent, vicious and dangerous but he wouldn't have come this far if he wasn't a smart strategist as well.

Jermaine 'Jay' Bennett – 18

T-Boy's lieutenant, Jay is a typical estate kid, none too bright and easily led. Hero worships T-Boy. He's fallen into a bad crowd and, if he toughens up a bit more, he could be as bad as his idol one day.

Once she has written her character analyses, Suzy puts them into a chart which will also include the dates the actors will be needed. She will use this to organize her information.

■ Example of breakdown chart

Now you know the qualities you are looking for, you can add that information to the practical requirements for each character. This is the information an agent or actor will need to know in order to decide if they might be able to play the part. Below we have used an example of the *Silent Witness* cast that Suzy described above.

CHARACTER	DATES	SPECIAL REQUIREMENTS	PLAYING AGE	GENDER	ETHNICITY	DESCRIPTION
Brenda	Shoot: 8 – 10 May	Motorcycle licence	Playing age range 25 to 30 – needs to realistically have a 13-year-old son	Female	Any	Attractive, in a sexy or tarty way. Has a warmth and likeability.
DS Dave Riley	Shoot: 8 – 12 May	Driving licence	Playing age early forties	Male	Mixed race	Could be mistakenly thought of as lazy but is very intelligent, deceptively laid-back. Good at his job. Relaxed manner.
T-Boy Thomas	Shoot: 9 – 12 May	Driving and motorcycle licence	Playing age range early to mid-twenties	Male	Any	Sharp, streetwise, tough, quite arrogant. A wheeler-dealer. Spikey.
Jermaine J. Bennet	Shoot: 10 – 12 May	Ability to rap/sing	Late teens	Male	Caribbean/black other areas	A follower not a leader. Lots of bravado and wants to come across tougher than he actually is. Nervy.

Exercise 6 – developing your breakdown

Using the chart below, do the same analysis for your script.

CHARACTER	DATES	SPECIAL REQUIREMENTS	PLAYING AGE	GENDER	ETHNICITY	DESCRIPTION

Once you have identified all the character and logistical information, you are ready to write the breakdown.

The breakdown is the first information sheet that the agent or actor will see. It must tell them everything they need to know in order to assess whether:

- the actor will *want* to do the part
  i.e. does the part sound challenging and interesting?

- the actor is *right* for the part
  i.e. is the character description something they are able to do?

- the actor *can* do the part
  i.e. are they **available**?

- the actor can *afford* to do the part
  i.e. will they be paid?

And crucially

- whether the actor is *excited* by the project
  i.e. who is involved and what is it for, does it sound unique, worthwhile, innovative, daring or fun?

Available/Availability
Whether an artist is free to work on specific dates for filming, rehearsals and/or performances.

WHAT YOU NEED TO PUT IN YOUR BREAKDOWN

A breakdown of the plot – be it theatre, film or television. Then very clear breakdowns for each role. We look at our client list first and foremost to see who is free for the dates – we're very keen on dates.

Jeremy Brook – agent

Go up
An actor being suggested for or suggesting themselves for a role.

All the relevant information needed for the actor or agent to make a decision as to whether to **go up** for the part has to be in your breakdown:

- Overall dates
  This should include any rehearsal period.

- Location
  If you are rehearsing at a different location, remember to specify.

■ Time commitment required
Some artists might only be needed for a couple of days over an entire filming period, or for many weeks for a theatre show.

■ Any payment or remuneration
What will the actor get for their work – either financial or otherwise?

■ **Synopsis**
Keep it brief and to the point but be sure to give the essence of the story.

Synopsis
A brief outline of the plot and characters of your script.

■ Character description
Identify qualities you are looking for.

■ When and where you will be casting for the project
Give details of dates, times and venue.

■ Who is involved and a brief background of the project
Is it a university/degree project or a small scale low budget film or a profit share? Give director/producer or company information.

■ Any other information
Are there sex scenes, nudity or anything else that the actor/ agent needs to know?

■ Deadline for CVs and applications

■ Contact information.

Here are two examples of how to lay out the necessary information to be circulated. One example is for a student film project and the other is for a small scale fringe theatre touring production.

We are using an imaginary production of *Romeo and Juliet* as an example and are initially looking to cast Romeo, Juliet and the Nurse. For the purposes of this exercise, we have created certain criteria for our characters.

CASTING BREAKDOWN – EXAMPLE STUDENT FILM

TITLE: *ROMEO and JULIET – A CONTEMPORARY RETELLING.*

OVERALL DATES: *1st – 15th May*

SHOOTING DATES: *3rd – 15th May*

LOCATION: *Cornwall – Penzance, UK*

FEE OR EXPENSES: *Expenses only plus travel and accommodation*

NAME OF DIRECTOR: *Sam Director*

NAME OF FILM SCHOOL: *Best Film School*

SYNOPSIS: A contemporary retelling of Shakespeare's *Romeo and Juliet* set in a regional town in Cornwall (Penzance). Juliet is the pampered daughter of Capulet, the local, much hated land-owner. Romeo is an extreme sports junkie whose family are old enemies of the Capulets.

CHARACTERS TO BE CAST:

JULIET   Female. Very striking, could look delicate but is in reality very feisty. She is overprotected and smothered and is longing to break free. Any ethnicity.

Playing range 15 – 19

ROMEO   Male. Very athletic. Active and quick. Agile. Loves a challenge. Any ethnicity. Playing range 18 – 20.

ANY OTHER INFORMATION: Must be able to free run and abseil.

NURSE   Has suffered early on in life, is a survivor, full of wisdom and a romantic. Any ethnicity or gender. Playing range thirties.

ANY OTHER INFORMATION: Should have a disability requiring a wheel-chair.

CONTACT DETAILS: *Jamie Producer*

DEADLINE DATE FOR CASTING SUBMISSIONS: *April 3rd*

DATES OF CASTING: *April 7 – 10th t.b.c.*

CASTING BREAKDOWN – EXAMPLE FRINGE THEATRE

TITLE: *ROMEO AND JULIET*

COMPANY: *Eire People's Theatre*

DATES OF REHEARSAL: *October 25th – November 30th*

DATES OF PERFORMANCES: *December 5th – January 30th*

LOCATION OF REHEARSALS: *Dublin*

LOCATION OF PERFORMANCES: *Touring*

FEE OR EXPENSES: *Profit Share*

NAME OF DIRECTOR: *Sam Director*

SYNOPSIS: A contemporary retelling of Shakespeare's *Romeo and Juliet*. Juliet is the pampered daughter of Capulet, the local, much hated land-owner. Romeo is an extreme sports junkie whose family are old enemies of the Capulets.

CHARACTERS TO BE CAST:

JULIET Female. Very striking, could look delicate but is in reality very feisty. Knowledge of Gaelic an advantage. Strong singing voice an advantage. Any ethnicity. Playing range 15 – 19.

ROMEO Male. Very athletic. Active and quick. Agile. Dance background an advantage. Any ethnicity. Playing range 18 – 20.

ANY OTHER INFORMATION: Must be able to breakdance.

NURSE Has suffered early on in life, is a survivor, full of wisdom and a romantic. Any ethnicity or gender. Playing range thirties.

ANY OTHER INFORMATION: Should have a disability requiring a wheel-chair.

CONTACT DETAILS: *Jamie Producer*

DEADLINE DATE FOR CASTING SUBMISSIONS: *October 1st*

DATES OF CASTING/WORKSHOPS: *During second week of October*

Casting breakdown template

Below is a template for you to fill in with details for casting your production.

CASTING BREAKDOWN

TITLE:

COMPANY:

DATES OF REHEARSAL:

DATES OF PERFORMANCES:

LOCATION OF REHEARSALS:

LOCATION OF PERFORMANCES:

FEE OR EXPENSES:

NAME OF DIRECTOR:

SYNOPSIS:

CHARACTERS TO BE CAST:

CONTACT DETAILS:
email:
phone:
fax:

DEADLINE DATE FOR CASTING SUBMISSIONS:

DATES OF CASTING/WORKSHOPS:

When should you send the breakdown out?

Four to five weeks before rehearsals or principal photography begins. It is unlikely that actors will be able to give a firm commitment to your dates any earlier than this.

One exception is if you are casting children under 16 years old as you *must* allow time for licensing. Please see Chapter 10 – Casting Children – for more detail on this.

The other exception is if you are approaching a well-known artist, which we will discuss in Chapter 3.

Case Study – the agent

Jeremy Brook *trained as an actor in 1988 and moved into working as an agent about ten years later. He now has his own agency – Jeremy Brook Ltd.*

JB: The most important asset you have as an agent is a very good client list. You've seen all their work, and can talk about them properly to casting directors, producers and directors. When I am making suggestions I want the producer or director to know 'That's Jeremy making that suggestion, so the actor will probably be very right for the role, so we'll try to get him or her in'.

The first thing I look for in a client is ability obviously – that has to be there straight away, and I try and watch as much TV, film and theatre as possible, to see what the trends are. It doesn't mean to say that I'm actually going out and looking for that, because it's the trend, but I'll go and see a drama school showcase and see a couple of people doing their stuff, being very good, and you know that is exactly the kind of thing they'll be seen for.

But I'll also see someone very good, whose 'castability' is less specific – so I have to think 'would they/could they segue into period drama, or could they do modern – like a regular part in *Coronation Street*?' I need to see how versatile they are.

Castability is a strange one for me because you sort of know when someone is very castable, but there are so many different things going on. You could have somebody who's very good theatrically and who you know could go into rep theatre doing Ibsen or Chekhov but, equally, they could suddenly end up getting a lead in *EastEnders*.

Q: Who are your most important relationships with? Casting directors, producers, writers or directors?

JB: In the first instance, it's casting directors – we'll nearly always deal with them first. The most important thing in the relationship with a casting director is trust, so that when you do pick up the phone to make a suggestion, they'll listen and they'll know that you're talking sense because they've dealt with you before.

Sometimes you will get a producer or director asking for a particular client, because they've worked with them before or because of profile or whatever it might be. But first and foremost it's the casting directors without question.

When we get a casting breakdown, or we know a play or read a script, we all have ideas about who would be right for that particular role – but sometimes they differ from the client's idea of themselves. I've got a good example – one of our boys, who's Turkish, wanted to be suggested for the role of Sinbad in *Sinbad* in a 12 part series for Sky. I didn't think he was right, based on the 'chocolate box' look that was suggested on the casting breakdown. I didn't think he had the athletics or the physique. I suggested him for another role – and then they got him in for Sinbad!

Q: What makes you advise your client to do a project?

JB: I'll always try and make sure the money's right – Equity deals on everything. If it isn't Equity, I leave it to the actor to decide. If the actor really likes the role, or the director, and if they want to do it, that's fine. But, I tell them that it needs to be a good fringe venue and that the role needs to be substantial – no point doing half a scene on the fringe. I'm happy for them to do fringe but not to waste time with something that's really not up there. Good new writing is the best thing for the fringe. And actors should at least get expenses, with some sort of token gesture on top of that.

Q: What advice would you give to no/low budget films/film students? What's the best way to approach your actors?

JB: If we're talking about the students, the best thing to do is to send an email with all the details – very particular details: dates, role, a copy of the script and say if you're interested in a particular actor.

Q: Would it have to be a firm offer?

JB: It doesn't need to be an offer, it's alright to ask for a meeting. Unless it's somebody with a bit more profile. As long as there are clear details. It's best if they've done a bit of work and picked out a particular actor whose work they might know or who they think might be very right for a particular role, then I'd look at it. Always send the script if you have it – so that we can get that sent to the actor straight away. It's quicker. I will always email back to say thanks, and that I'll send it on to the particular actor and will come back as soon as I know.

I've had Spotlight Link things from the National Film and Television School, Bournemouth Film School and London Met. Rather than asking me to make suggestions on a film school breakdown, if they have done some work and ask for one of our actors by name, I prefer it. Because if you're busy and you get a film school breakdown through, for expenses only, or Equity 65 quid a day, if you're really, really busy – sometimes you'll just delete it.

Q: Any other conditions?

JB: Well, look after the actor wherever the filming takes place. If they're not being picked up – which I know they can't afford – then all expenses should be covered. Give clear calls and, particularly if it's expenses only, it's very important that they know where they're going; how to get there; call time; a very clear schedule.

They need somewhere to go to relax, they need feeding and watering properly and they need to be spoken to – they can't be left in the dark. If anything goes wrong and timings go by the board – which they do, we all know that – then the actors need to know what's happening. Common courtesy really – I've had people just having a nightmare.

Q: And what about the after care?

JB: Ha! I've had to chase DVDs. And it's irritating. Part of the reason for doing it is to get the DVD, especially the young ones, who haven't had any television or film experience. They use them to put together a showreel and on their Spotlight Link – so that's why it's important. The students should be as professional with the actors as the professional actors are being with them.

CHAPTER 3

WHERE TO LOOK FOR YOUR CAST

- What is an agent and what do they do?
- Who represents whom?
- How to contact an agent
- Finding cast through personal contacts
- Casting methods to be wary of
- ☐ Case study – the freelance casting director

■ WHERE TO LOOK FOR YOUR CAST

We have talked about the kind of research you should do to prepare for casting, including watching TV, film and theatre. It is possible that high profile, experienced actors would be willing to work with you – if you approach them in the right way. Whether or not you have a specific actor in mind, you will need to approach an agent at some point during the casting process.

WHAT IS AN AGENT AND WHAT DO THEY DO?

An agent's job is to be a bit of go between. That's really all it is. I would hope that we have nurtured the relationships with directors, producers and casting directors, in order for them to trust our judgement. It's a very human job, hugely dependent on collaboration and conversation.

Megan Wheldon – agent, Lou Coulson Associates

Actors have agents to represent their interests. The agent negotiates fees and conditions, guides their career, advises them on decisions, knows their strengths and weaknesses, their likes and dislikes, their dreams and ambitions. Very often, an agent has first seen their client when they were at drama school, or in a fringe or student performance.

They can become partners with other agents, increase their client list and sometimes take on writers, directors and producers, and become involved in the packaging of projects.

Agents care about their clients and are there to enable them to do great work, to build their careers – and to facilitate them in making a living in this most difficult of professions.

They also have to earn a living and are running their businesses to make a profit. At the most basic level, their income is derived from the commission they take from any work that they find for an actor.

Remember, if you are asking an actor to work for minimum, or profit share or no money, then you are also asking the agent for a favour too.

You don't just take on the actor, you take on the person.

Victoria Futcher – agent, Lou Coulson Associates

WHO REPRESENTS WHOM?

It is not difficult to discover an actor's agent. It is worth joining **IMDb Pro,** as actors' agents, managers and publicists are all listed. In the UK you can search **Spotlight,** on their database which lists every actor who is a member and the details of their agent. If the actor doesn't have an agent, but is a member of Spotlight, then you can contact them through Spotlight, who will pass on your details. In the US, **SAG** will tell you who the actor's agent is.

IMDB Pro (subscription required)
Has in-depth information of actors' managers, agents, and contact details for individuals and companies

Spotlight is a great resource. We interviewed Pippa Harrison, head of Spotlight's client relations:

SPOTLIGHT
A UK directory of actors and actresses

WHAT IS SPOTLIGHT?

Spotlight started in 1927, it was a like a pamphlet with about a hundred performers in it with their photograph and their contact details. We now have over 40,000 members of Spotlight so our actors and actresses book is currently ten volumes at the moment. Every member appears in our books and on our website (*www.spotlight.com*). Casting directors can search the database, they can also send out casting breakdowns via the Spotlight Link. The majority of work cast in the UK is sent out on the Spotlight Link.

SAG-AFTRA
Screen Actors' Guild and American Federation of TV and Radio Artists (USA) – Actors' union that has agreements in place for actors working in all recorded media.

The important thing about Spotlight is that you can only appear in Spotlight if you have trained at a recognized drama school or if you have professional experience. You don't have to be an Equity member to go into Spotlight, but if two people want to join Spotlight with the same name, the preference will go to the Equity member with the name.

Spotlight is part of The International Alliance of Casting Directories (*www.iacd.com*), a global organization which includes Spotlight in the UK, Breakdown Services in America and Showcase in Australia.

What is the Spotlight Link?

The Spotlight Link is the quickest and easiest way for casting directors and production companies to get their casting breakdowns into the in-boxes of leading UK agents and performers.

Universities and colleges can subscribe to Spotlight and it is an invaluable tool for students casting their productions

☐   How does spotlight work?

You can post a breakdown on Spotlight Link:

■   to all agents
■   to agents of your choice
■   to the Spotlight Link Board and it will be seen by all agents and performers who are members of Spotlight.

Agents will receive the breakdown in their in-box and, if they have available artists who fit your breakdown description, they will contact you with suggestions. Unrepresented actors who appear in Spotlight receive casting breakdowns through the Spotlight Link Board.

A subscription will also mean you can receive the hardback directories, which are broken down into specific categories. There are categories for:

■   children
■   young performers
■   dancers
■   presenters
■   actresses
■   actors
■   stunt performers
■   graduates.

Other casting websites and networks

In the UK, Spotlight is the main professional tool for casting, but there are many others including those that are regionally specific.

If you have a specific actor in mind for a role, the first step is to contact their agent.

HOW TO CONTACT AN AGENT

Contacts
Published by Spotlight – contains listings for over 5000 companies, services and individuals across all branches of TV, stage, film and radio.

You can find contact details for all UK agents in **CONTACTS** which is published by Spotlight. Once you have found the number or email address, resist the temptation to immediately launch into a sales pitch of your project.

The first thing you have to find out is if the actor is available for your dates. A phone call to the agent will let you know if their client is available. If they are available, you need to know whether they would be prepared to do it.

☐   Example of a phone conversation with an agent to
     check availability

```
INT. PRODUCTION OFFICE - DAY

YOU pick up the phone and dial the AGENT of the actor you are
interested in casting for your project.

                    YOU
          Hello, my name is (insert your
          name) and I am calling from (insert
          your company/university/course)  I
          wanted to check (insert actor's
          name) availability and interest in
          my short film/theatre piece.  Could
          you tell me who I should speak to
          please?

                    AGENT
          You can talk to me - what are the
          dates?

                    YOU
          Great, could you tell me your name?

                    AGENT
          Sure, I'm XXX.

                    YOU
          Thanks.  The overall dates are XXX
          and it will be filming/rehearsing
          in (name of location)  We would
          need him/her for XX days in all.

                    AGENT
          Is there a fee?

                    YOU
          We're only able to offer expenses
          for this as well as a DVD of the
          film.
          OR
          Yes, we're able to offer a nominal
          fee of XXX.
          OR
          Yes, we are paying the Equity
          Fringe fee of XXX per week/job
          OR
          We are all on profit share for this
          job.

                    AGENT
          Yes he/she is available for your
          dates.  I'd need to check whether
          he/she would be interested in doing
          it for that fee.  Could you email
          us the script?

                    YOU
          That'd be great.  What's your email
          address?
```

You shouldn't expect a very experienced or well known actor to read or audition for you. In the very lucky scenario that they love your script, and want to do the role, the most you can expect is that they will agree to meet you for a chat, so that they can size you up. You are going to have to offer them the role at the same time as you send them the script.

Offer
Terms that are proposed to an actor or their agent regarding a specific job.

We asked Megan Wheldon and Victoria Futcher from Lou Coulson Associates, how they liked to be approached about their clients.

MW: The best way – if it's the director - is to approach the agent first, because we hold the diary. And also I don't think agents take kindly to people not having done their research, not knowing what their clients are doing or who their clients are. It's much better and it avoids any confusion, if they approach us.

Q: With what?

MW: If they are after a high profile client, the thing not to do is to ask them to come and audition for a student film. I mean we will send out showreels and certainly send our student graduates.

Q: Rule number two is?

VF: Send us the script, give us all the information, even if there's no money – you know, everyone understands, especially right now.

MW: They do want to help up-and-coming directors.

VF: Rather than trying to be cagey because they think we're going to say no, give us all the information up front.

MW: And I absolutely think they must do their homework and be aware of status.

Sample agent letter/email

Dear   *(agent's name – correctly spelt)*

(Title of piece)   by   *(writer)*

(Name of actor)

Following on from our conversation earlier this morning/this week/on *(the date)* , please find enclosed/attached the script of   *(title of script)* . I am also sending/attaching a brief biography of myself and other members of the creative team, so you can get an idea of our background and our hopes for the script.

I am the director/producer of the film/play and we would love to offer the role of   *(name of character)*   to   *(name of actor)*   as I really feel that he/she would be wonderful in the part and I would love the opportunity to work with them.

As I mentioned on the phone, we are able to offer expenses and a DVD of the finished piece/a nominal fee of/expenses only/Equity fringe contract on this project. We would do our best to accommodate the other commitments of   *(actor's name)*.

Just to reiterate the details: We will be filming/rehearsing from   *(date)* to *(date)* . We will be filming/rehearsing in   *(name of town/region)* .

Once you and   *(name of actor)*   have had a chance to read the script, it would be wonderful to organize a coffee and a chat with   *(name of actor)*   to discuss the project further.

I will ring/email your office in a couple of days to make sure you have received this safely.

Many thanks for all your help,

With best wishes,

(Your name)

Checklist for making an offer to an actor:

- Ask the agent if you can submit your script and who to address it to.

see Appendices 'Scripts'

- Ensure that your script is presented in the **industry standard format**.

- Write a covering letter that introduces yourself, your project, the part you are offering and why you are offering it to this particular artist.

- Keep it to one side of A4 and be clear and honest.

- Package it up, send it off and wait.

Give it two weeks and then email or call and ask if it was received. If no one in the office knows anything about it, be prepared to send the whole package off again.

Wait another week, call again. If there is still no response, try an email asking for feedback or an answer one way or the other. Before moving on you need to be sure that the actor is definitely saying 'no' or you need to be clear that you have withdrawn your offer. It would be deeply embarrassing if you assumed a 'no' only for the actor to come back with a 'yes', after you'd offered it to someone else.

If the artist says 'yes' the next step is for you to arrange to meet. Try and find somewhere reasonably quiet and relaxed where you can buy them a cup of coffee.

Here is an example of a confirmation email that you should send prior to the meeting.

Dear (*name of agent*)

Further to our email/phone conversation, please find the details of the meeting with (*name of actor*) with myself and the producer/director/ writer (*delete as appropriate*).

We look forward to seeing him/her on (*day and date of meeting*) at (*time of meeting*) at (*venue and postcode if necessary*).

Best wishes,

(*your name & contact number*)

If the meeting is not in a public place, it is always courteous to write down directions as well as sending the postcode, i.e. what is the nearest/most convenient train/tube/bus stop – what is the best route and how long it takes to walk. Also put in whether there is a car park/free parking nearby.

Be sure to tell them who will be at the meeting. Ensure that the agent has a contact number in case something goes wrong at their end. Ensure that you have the agent's number in case something goes wrong at your end.

You *cannot* be late for the meeting. And make sure you are prepared. Below is a checklist to help you remember everything.

A checklist for meeting with the artist

Send out clear directions for the meeting – including a Google reference if appropriate.	
Give the agent your contact number.	
Have a contact number for the actor's agent with you.	
Have a copy of the script with you and any other details you might need – e.g. mood board or synopsis/ideas.	
Get to the meeting place half an hour ahead of time to secure a table and make sure it is not too noisy for your meeting, especially if the meeting is in a public cafe.	
Have enough money with you to pay for a beverage for the actor and yourselves.	
Set a time limit for the meeting – an hour maximum.	
Have a list of questions prepared to ask/get the conversation going.	

By being on time you show that you are professional, organized and focussed both on the project and on them. It shows you are committed and prepared, so that the actor will feel confident that you know what you are doing. You want them to look forward to working with you because the initial chat was enjoyable and well run.

If you are late, it shows a lack of respect, organization and time management and could mean that the actor decides not to do your project. You must be early. Ready. Prepared. Know what you want to talk about and be honest in answering any questions that they may have.

If you land your first choice of actor, you can stop long enough to give yourself a pat on the back – and then get back to work.

PERSONAL CONTACTS

This is a valid place to start. You may have met an actor on a production, in whatever capacity you were working, you really liked what they did and you think they would be great for your project.

> *'After I'd done Confetti, I went and did a telly and there was a supporting artist who'd written a script – he'd liked Confetti and asked if I would consider doing his script and I said, "I always work through my agent, but I wouldn't not consider doing it!" And he said "we're already talking to Sir Norman Wisdom" And there were some amazing people who'd given a morning of their time.'*
>
> Vincent Franklin – actor

The John Travolta Tactic – sophisticated high risk strategy casting

Quentin Tarantino approached John Travolta to be in Pulp Fiction when Travolta's career was languishing. What was so clever about this piece of casting is that at the time what Travolta was most famous for was the sexy, high school, dancing hunk of Grease. However, in *Pulp Fiction* he was cast as a slightly overweight, flabby, heroin-using hit man. But what Travolta had in both of these wildly opposing genres was his charisma and his sense of 'cool', which comes through despite the character. It was this juxtaposition that Tarantino so cleverly realized would work. Travolta leapt at the chance. Result.

WAYS OF CASTING TO BE WARY OF:

Getting your mates in is not a good option. You may have a mate who fancies themselves as a bit of an actor but, unless they have some acting experience, they are unlikely to be able to take direction and give you options that will make your production the best it can be. You need actors who can take direction, bring their own ideas, offer you choices and who will enable you to raise your game, and learn how to communicate and collaborate with professionals.

A professional actor doesn't just do it once and that's it, they understand that the job requires that they repeat a line, a move or a scene as often as is necessary for the director to get what is needed. They will remember their emotional arc from one scene to the next.

Your flatmate or street cast 'real' person will get very weary when asked to repeat a master shot, a two shot, close ups and reverses and it is extremely unlikely that they will be able to reproduce their performance successfully from one take to the next.

Street casting is a risky and unpredictable casting technique. There are always stories about how a director or producer cast a great busker in the street, the baker who fed the film crew or a cab driver with a great turn of phrase. However, remember that it is hard enough for a seasoned director to work like this whilst for the inexperienced or novice director it will make the task ten times harder.

Street casting
Looking in non-professional environments for non-actors to become part of your project.

..in the end, the bottom line is, it's about acting and actors acting and the sophisticated thing called acting
                                        Mike Leigh - director

Case Study – the freelance casting director

Kate Rhodes James is a freelance casting director who is passionate about her creative role in the development of a wide range of projects.

KRJ: I need to love a script and respond to it immediately. I know when I'm onto something good when I need to grab a pen and paper to start jotting down ideas. I need to feel inspired and excited. If I'm reading a script and nobody is springing to mind, that's the warning sign that this is not for me. If I don't believe in it, I can't sell it to the agent/actor.

I would then meet the director and hope that we get on and have the same vision. Sometimes we don't and it goes no further.

Q: So the personal relationships of that team are key?

KRJ: Oh, it's imperative. Whenever I meet a director, I always ask 'what is your vision? What is your ambition for the piece?' This way I can ensure that I will deliver the kind of actor that is right for their piece. I make it clear that the creative process is very important to me and I will say if I think we are going in the wrong direction. The best directors are collaborative. I have just worked with a director who allowed me to drive the audition if I knew an actor was misreading his direction. He was really happy for me to contribute. That for me is the perfect union between a casting director and a director. Directors need to understand that we know the actors better than they do and they must fully utilize that.

Once I've been offered the job, I have a coffee with the director – usually one to one – and discuss the roles thoroughly. Good writing will always allow interpretation, so you can have stimulating and fun discussions. Once we have ascertained how the roles will be described I draw up a breakdown and issue it to the all the relevant agents.

Sometimes a lot of directors don't know really what they want, and they need to be guided. Once trust has been established between the casting director and the director – and sometimes it doesn't happen – you can then go 'off-piste' and that's when the fun happens and great ideas come about. When you suddenly suggest someone who is not as the role is written, but contributes to the plot and the relationship with another character, it becomes really exciting. That's when the fun begins.

My advice to young directors would be, right at the beginning, maybe before you've even gone into prep, spend a good few hours having lunch with your casting director, getting to know them a bit and allowing them to get to know you. Personally, I like to find out who they find inspiring. A director who I worked with was inspired by Milos Foreman. That told me a lot about him, his influences.

Casting directors are creatives and a lot of people in the industry don't understand that. The skill of our job is not necessarily the knowledge but what we do with our knowledge. That is the skill. It's hard to quantify what we do. I am very instinctive, as a lot are. I just know when someone is right. It shouldn't matter that they weren't very good in something earlier, if they deliver in the room, and make sense of the world that we are in, then that is your lead.

Q: What are your key relationships?

KRJ: My key relationships? It is controversial but people need to know that one of our key relationships is with agents. The relationship with the casting director and agent is imperative. It has to be based on trust and we have to be honest. I can't achieve what I want to achieve for their client unless they work with me.

There was a wonderful agent who has since given up the business. She phoned me after reading a breakdown of *Bleak House*. She urged me to meet this young actress who had done very little but she was convinced she was my Ada. As I had a great working relationship with this agent, I went for it, and thankfully that young actress was Carey Mulligan. She was the first actress through the door and the first to read for Ada and no one came near after that. There are some directors who wouldn't have taken the risk, but Justin Chadwick is not risk averse and neither am I. The producer, was a bit nervous of giving a role to someone so inexperienced but Justin said, 'don't worry, we'll do it.' And he did.

Q: And did you then have to see lots more, considering she was the first one up?

KRJ: Well, no – our producer was of the old school, he didn't want time wasted seeing hundreds of people. He employed a casting director to cut through all that. We certainly saw a few because even for me, it seemed too good to be true, right at the beginning of the process that we had found her! And also, that's another indication of how Justin and I got on, he trusted me implicitly to do my job. When I said 'Look, I'm going to bring in this girl – sight unseen' he said, 'Fine, go for it!'

So my advice to a young director would be, make a friend out of your casting director. We all nurture our relationships with directors and once that bond has been made it's a great reassurance to you. We also make you look very, very good!

CHAPTER 4

CASTING DIRECTORS

■ Who employs the casting director?

■ When are casting directors employed?

■ Where to find casting directors?

■ How to become a casting director?

☐ Case study – the auteur and the casting director

■ CASTING DIRECTORS

The relationship that you have with the casting director is as essential as the relationships that you have with the director of photography or producer – it's essential to the end product and it's very collaborative.

Damien Goodwin – director

Even if you have no budget you can still approach a casting director for help and advice. If you do have a budget, and are paying fees, minimum wage or giving a percentage of profits, then the casting director should be treated in exactly the same way as all your other company or crew members.

If you are thinking of approaching a casting director, watch their work and identify what it is that makes you want to collaborate with them. There should be some affinity between their work and your production and the type of cast you are looking for: perhaps you have two children to cast and they have a lot of experience with casting children, or they regularly work with a director you particularly admire.

If you are lucky enough to find one who is willing to help you, be flexible and open to the casting director's ideas – don't just go to them hoping they can access a **name** for you.

Name
An actor with profile and track record of well-known acting work.

WHAT IS A CASTING DIRECTOR?

The really good casting director can find the perfect actor for that role, sometimes the only actor who could play that role.

Jason O'Mara – actor

Head of department (HOD)
In charge of an area of production.

The role of casting director, is a **head of department (HOD)** position. They match the demands of the script with the qualities and attributes of the actor and oversee, and take responsibility for, all the organization and administration concerned with the casting process and the employment of the actors.

WHAT DO THEY DO?

Casting directors are ultimately here to be efficient and to save everybody's time.

Kate Rhodes James – casting director

Casting directors cast the speaking roles. They don't just cast the **leads** and generally are not responsible for casting non-speaking roles. In theatre they often cast the understudies.

Lead/s
The pivotal character/s in a script.

> *They are the ones that get you in the door.*
>
> Angela Lonsdale – actor

Casting directors watch actors' work on stage or on screen and have a thorough working knowledge of emerging talent. They also attend drama school showcases. This is where the graduate actors perform one or two minute speeches in various genres, as well as in short scene extracts, and may possibly sing and dance as well. Casting directors also attend many full length final year productions, to see the actors perform a sustained character in a play or musical.

Casting directors research actors and know their career history.

> *I think it always helps if you know the director or casting director because they know what you're capable of.*
>
> Ruby Snape – actor

Casting directors develop working relationships with agents.

> *I think it's possibly the most important relationship, as the casting director is who you work with most of the time and all you have is that relationship that you build up – if it works and you get on and you can trust each other.*
>
> Victoria Futcher – agent, Lou Coulson Associates

Casting directors keep up to date with current television, film and theatre.

> *There's a sense with casting directors that some of them are really creative in the process – Nina Gold would be one of those – she came to see me in a play and I got the Mike Leigh off the back of that.*
>
> Vincent Franklin – actor

Casting Directors are to be found in the audience of theatres up and down the country. Sometimes they are there as a guest of an agent who has a client in the play, or because they are researching a project, or they are simply keeping an eye on who's doing what and where. They will visit every type of theatre from major companies to fringe and everything in between.

I know that they're out and about looking and constantly searching not just casting off the television screen.

Diana Kyle – producer

Casting directors have creative discussions with the director and/or the producer.

What show are we making? Who is it for? What's the demographic? What are the particularities with it? Are we inheriting some cast? What are our initiatives for new casting?

Tim Bradley – TV producer

Casting directors start by reading the script and begin thinking of actors who would be interesting to put forward, based on the brief from the producer.

On board
Anyone who has agreed terms and is committed to a project.

*It was around 180 characters. Nobody was **on board**. We cast every single person. We absolutely were given a very specific brief which is, 'we want popular faces in there'. We took that.*

Kate Rhodes James – casting director

Casting directors talk through initial ideas based on their instinct, knowledge and experience; coupled with ideas from the director and producer.

One thing I sometimes say is 'Oh, somebody a bit like that', but that's really just to start a conversation and it's often not necessarily the right thing, but it's very useful because then you suddenly jump onto one characteristic or one particular element.

Tim Bradley – TV producer

Some directors have a huge knowledge base of actors and some don't at all – or they do but they can't remember any names – you get those wonderful descriptions, you know, "oh, it was her!"

Nadine Rennie – casting director

Casting directors:

- write and distribute the breakdown
- talk to agents, check availabilities
- draw up availability lists
- shortlist choices with the director/producer
- arrange and run casting sessions.

'If I was a producer, I would be employing a casting director to show me the best actors available for the role – all different shapes

and sizes – and then if we haven't got it, we'll know it's because we've missed a beat in the script.'

Kate Rhodes James– casting director

After the casting session the team will discuss the actors seen and decide who to offer the roles to. However, depending on the medium, this can involve several levels of decision makers. Very often there will be different ideas, views or agendas on casting.

Same part, ten different ways of playing it.

Jean Diamond – agent

It may be necessary to re-think a role after a casting session has taken place. The casting director will then have to draw on their experience to find new suggestions for the role.

A casting director is invaluable. They are constantly offering hundreds and hundreds of competent actors – very good actors – who they know. They understand the business.

Diana Kyle – producer

If necessary, the casting director will arrange **recalls**. In television, there are often many rounds of recalls, so that different executives can see the creative team's choice of actor.

Recall
Asking an actor to a further meeting to audition and/or read for the same role.

You leave the room, everyone loves you, you think you've got the job, then three people down the line decide on a different person to play the wife/husband, who doesn't match you and the job goes to someone else.

Jean Diamond – agent

The casting director keeps the actor and actors' agents up to date with the casting process.

This is not as easy as it sounds as a lot of the time the casting director simply won't have a definitive answer to the simple question of 'have they got the job?' Sometimes an actor will get another offer making the whole process more complicated, especially if the decision is taking a long time. The casting director has to keep all the plates spinning.

For a new regular character I would give as much information as I could. And the casting director would offer me a short list of say, 25 well-respected actors.... Ultimately, it's about who's available, who's willing to come and work on the program and then who's the best actor for that part.

Diana Kyle – producer

The casting director makes the offers and books the actors once the casting decisions have been made. In some cases a key actor has to be offered the role and their deal has to be negotiated and agreed, before the casting director can offer to the rest of the cast, as everything is dependent on who is playing the key role.

> *Sometimes you've got to take one character and focus hard before the others can fall into place.*
>
> Tim Bradley – producer

Locked
Confirmed shooting dates.

In theatre, actors are employed for the whole rehearsal and performance period. However, in television and film, until the shooting schedule has been **locked** the actors cannot be booked.

The casting director negotiates the deal and terms for the actors. This includes both the financial offer and working conditions. Sometimes the casting director has their own budget, or will work in conjunction with the producer. They need to have a working knowledge of the various industry agreements.

Negotiations can be rigorous and should be conducted with good will and understanding on both sides. Honesty and transparency are essential when negotiating and budgeting – actors talk amongst themselves and if they discuss their fees, and discover that another actor is being paid on a different scale than that which the casting director had said was possible, it can create bad feeling and poor working relationships. This can only damage the production.

Casting advice note (also can be known as the deal memo)
Information and contact sheet including any financial agreement.

The casting director produces the **casting advice note**. This is the tangible form of what has been verbally agreed until the contract is generated and signed. It is very important that all the information on the casting advice note is correct and everyone agrees it and signs off on it.

The casting advice note goes to the associate producer or producer to be double-checked and then is sent to the agent.

> *The casting director is as much a head of department on a show as any other HOD. It's a full time industry.*
>
> Tim Bradley – TV producer

The casting director can generate the contract for television, theatre and film productions.

It is the mix between searching for something as part of the creative process and having good administration skills, being able to organize sessions and look at logistics.

Hannah Miller – Head of casting RSC

Often final casting decisions are not made until close to the first day of rehearsal or principal photography, so it is important that the casting director is in contact with the relevant departments – especially make-up and wardrobe.

The casting director keeps a watching brief during production. Once principal photography or rehearsals begin, the bulk of the casting director's job will have been completed. However, they remain involved as there may still be roles that need casting, or an actor may become injured or ill and need replacing. All of this comes under the auspices of a 'watching brief' and in fact the casting director can only really breathe a sigh of relief once the production has wrapped and they are standing at the wrap party several months later.

WHO EMPLOYS THE CASTING DIRECTOR?

The casting director is genuinely a significant part of the creative quality of the project and indeed nearly all the films that I've done – certainly the vast majority of them – the casting directors have been responsible for bringing in amazing ensembles.

Marc Samuelson – film producer

Very often directors and producers develop a relationship with one casting director, who becomes a vital part of their creative team.

■ in film, the production company (the producer or executive producer) employs the casting director

■ in regional theatre the director of the play in consultation with the artistic or executive director of the theatre

■ in commercial theatre, the producer

■ in television, if it is an independent production, then it will be the production company, in consultation with the producer, director and possibly with the approval of the network. If it is an in-house production (e.g. *EastEnders*, *Casualty*, *Doctors*), there is a resident casting team where one casting director will be responsible for a block or series of episodes, overseen by the head of casting.

WHEN ARE CASTING DIRECTORS EMPLOYED?

Part of the joy of having a casting director is working with collaborators who make it better. I haven't got the best ideas in the world, I'm very aware of that, people come up with better ideas, and then I can pretend that I come up with them.

J Blakeson – director

In independent film casting directors are often brought onto the production at an early development stage. Their involvement can be vital in securing the talent that will bring funding to the project.

In major studio films, lead actors are often attached long before the casting director is on board.

In television drama they are generally employed between four and twelve weeks before filming commences.

Knowledge of actors in the UK – also using the generally great tool of Spotlight to prompt you by putting in various searches. But it's my knowledge base, it's me going out there and seeing things three or four times a week, showcases, meeting actors for generals, watching at least the first episode of every new series, just maintaining that knowledge; reading reviews, who's doing what, who's got great reviews. It's my knowledge and my job to put that list together.

Nadine Rennie – casting director

WHERE TO FIND CASTING DIRECTORS?

www.thecdg.co.uk

You will find their details on IMDB, in CONTACTS and, if they are a member, on the **Casting Directors Guild website**. Most casting directors are freelance practitioners and work in all areas of the industry. Some are well known for their expertise in a specific area. For example, David Grindrod is well known for his work on major West End and touring musicals, whilst Nina Gold is better known for her work on feature films.

In-house
A casting person or department that is employed full time by a company.

In the USA, many TV and film studios have **in-house** casting departments, whilst in the UK this is not so common. In British theatre, the RSC, the National, the Royal Court Theatre and the Donmar Warehouse have resident casting departments, although most theatre producers hire casting directors on a freelance, project-by-project basis.

Many great casting directors can handle all kinds of genres, and take on the specific creative approach of different directors for different films. And yet still if you pay attention, I think you can always discern the subtle signature a great casting director can bring to the work.

James Schamus – film producer/writer

HOW TO BECOME A CASTING DIRECTOR?

There is no one route to becoming a casting director. Every casting director we interviewed for this book came into it from very different beginnings: through training as an actor, theatre stage management, theatre directing, working for a casting director or agent. What they all have in common is a huge interest and delight in actors and their work, a background knowledge in theatre or film and a very good memory for names.

The best way to become a casting director, as Jean Diamond wisely points out, is to learn and get experience. See as much theatre as you can, watch TV drama, go to see movies – taking particular note of British films and actors if you are based in the UK whilst being aware of what's going on in Europe and the US, ensuring a broad understanding of the industry you want to join. Immerse yourself in the world so you know who's who: casting directors, directors and producers. Pursue work experience to discover if you enjoy the work. Look on the CDG website to find out who is currently casting what, reference IMDB to learn the names of the casting directors whose work you like and appreciate.

The only way to become an agent is to be an assistant and learn on the job – and it's the same with casting

Jean Diamond – agent

Case Study – the auteur and the casting director

Mike Leigh and Nina Gold CDG *have worked together on many productions. Their relationship is a wonderful example of how a multi-award winning, uncompromising director – with a unique, individual approach – is so keenly aware of the importance of casting, that he insisted we interview him together with Nina.*

ML: I'm very happy to talk about my idiosyncratic work, but I think the most important thing is to distinguish between the method, such as it is, and the approach or attitude – and so address the wider application of the particular kind of things that I do.

When somebody comes into this room for an initial interview, it's never scheduled for less than 20 minutes. And there's never anyone else in the room. If I'm going to work with an actor and find a language that only that actor and I speak, from the word 'go' it's got to be private. And having somebody else in the room puts unnecessary pressure on the conversation.

And – this is very important indeed – when I'm at the casting stage of one of my projects, I usually have no idea what it is. The meeting isn't to do with me and my project. So, what do we talk about in that 20 minutes? We talk about them! Not about me, they know about me. We talk about them and their work and their personal life and I give them some space to be themselves.

After the initial conversation, if I want to pursue it, I then call them back for an hour. Again, one to one with nobody else there, and we actually do a bit of work on character of some kind. But with my stuff – and again it sits at one end of the spectrum – it is absolutely all about character acting. It's all about people not just playing themselves. One is not looking for raw personalities whom the character will then become. We are talking about actors who are versatile and intelligent and sophisticated and witty and have some sense of society and all of those things.

NG: Also it's worth pointing out that unlike practically everybody, you don't tape them.

ML: Putting the actor on tape would be an enormous distraction, a complete waste of time and as far as I'm concerned the minute you have a camera there you are, however much you tell yourself you're not, you are at some level creating an artefact and we are in the business of not doing that. We're doing something that is organic and immediate and in the moment, and it's about making things up, finding things out, research.

NG: In fact, even when they get the part it's going to be hell of a long time before the camera gets involved.

ML: Yes, I never tape rehearsal, ever, never! Once, I did for 20 minutes in 1966 and I chucked it out of the window!

NG: Because they need to be fully right there with their character before they're ready to move on.

ML: At this stage there is no question of who or what the character is. I am looking for a versatile actor and once I know that person is on board then I can collaborate with them to find something very interesting and make it happen. Plainly our way of casting is very idiosyncratic but what I do that has an application in all types of casting is to work backwards from what is there.

NG: A lot of people want the actor to walk in the door and present them with the ready made, perfect version of the character that the director has in their mind by random fluke really.

ML: Without any work.

NG: Yes, without any real work, or starting point.

ML: So, following on from that, one of the great occupational hazards of all of this is that actors, because of the normal conventions of having just to turn up on set and do it, and because their agent says 'Well, wear this.', or 'Lose weight for that.'. It makes actors behave in completely bizarre and unnatural ways and creates bad habits.

NG: It also means things happening like when you ask the question 'How old are you?' an actor answering 'How old would you like me to be?'

ML: In a word, 'hope', gets in the way and it grabs you, and the poor actor becomes more and more confused, because of the conditions of the industry which makes them have to be instant.

NG: It really gets in the way of the process and stops them doing the proper acting.

ML: Absolutely, so acting takes the back seat to a whole lot of other stuff.

Q: You end up trying to be what you think they want you to be.

NG: Yes, and they give you no input on telling you what that is, so the actor doesn't know and actually nobody knows, which is why you get situations where the director says, 'Well, no actually, I don't really like that actor' and each person you present them with 'doesn't feel quite right' and that's because nothing *is* quite right.

ML: And that comes back to my point of working back from what there is.

NG: One of the things that makes Mike really good at casting is that he's been out there looking at actors practically every night in the theatre for years, and he's got an incredibly wide ranging, detailed knowledge of British actors.

ML: (*To NG*) Much helped by your even wider knowledge of this.

NG: Yes, but you know a lot and you take an active interest in discovering what people are doing and what they are all about, which is a great starting point for directors who really want to figure out how to do casting.

ML: The bottom line is, that there is no question that anybody wanting to cast actors has to be involved with theatre at some point, even if only as a visitor. And if we're talking about young directors then they do need to get their asses in gear and look at stuff.

Chapter 5

CVs, SHOWREELS AND PLANNING THE SESSION

- How to Read a CV
- Watching a Showreel
- Deciding who to see
- What sort of session to do
- Which scenes to choose
- Audition exercises
- ☐ Case study – the artistic director

■ CVS, SHOWREELS AND PLANNING THE SESSION

It's coming from the character – because actually what we're looking for is a girl with a pretty but not glam model attractive face – not cut-glass lines but homely and lovely with a soft edge and regional accent because we don't want her to be seen as posh – so already in my head I'm building a character.

Tim Welton – director/producer

At this point, you will have completed your breakdown, posted it on the relevant websites and sent it to appropriate agents. Now you will begin to get suggestions of actors for the roles. This will be in the form of **CVs** (referred to as resumes in the US), which will include **head shots** and **showreels**.

Head shots
Professionally taken photograph of an actor.

Showreels
Selections of an actor's on-screen work, edited together.

CV
A list of all the acting credits, and relevant skills, of an actor.

It is important to get used to reading a **CV** in order to find out as much as you can about the actor and the work that they have done. On the pages that follow we show you some examples of CVs to give you an idea of the different types of layout you can expect:

■ a CV taken from the Spotlight directory:

Notes:

Photo: Jenny Potter

FLEUR CHANDLER
Spotlight Actresses 2011/2012
Page 691

AMANDA SAROSI ASSOCIATES
1 Holmbury View, London E5 9EG
Phone: 020-7993 6008
Fax: 020-7096 2141
E-mail: amanda@asassociates.biz

Location:	London	**Hair Colour:**	Red/Titian
Height:	5'5" (165cm)	**Hair Length:**	Short
Playing Age:	46 - 60 years	**Voice Character:**	Assured
Role Types:	Eastern European, White	**Voice Quality:**	Clear
Eye Colour:	Blue		
Equity			

Credits:

Stage

2009, Stage, Mrs Gardiner, PRIDE AND PREJUDICE, Theatre Royal Bath, Toby Frow

2009, Stage, Mary, CANCER TALES, Trevor Walker

2008, Stage, Lady Bracknell, THE IMPORTANCE OF BEING ERNEST, Middle Ground Theatre, Michael Lunney

Stage, CORIOLANUS, HENRY VI, TIS PITY SHE'S A WHORE, DANCE OF DEATH, Royal Shakespeare Company

Stage, Lady Bracknell, THE IMPORTANCE OF BEING EARNEST, Harrogate, Andrew Manley

Stage, Gertrude, HAMLET, Harrogate, Andrew Manley

2003, Stage, Ase, PEER GYNT, Arcola Theatre, David Levin

1999, Stage, Amanda, THE GLASS MENAGERIE, Ipswich Wolsey Theatre, Andrew Manley

1997, Stage, Muriel, SOLDIERING ON - TALKING HEADS, Ipswich Wolsey Theatre, Andrew Manley

1993, Stage, Lady Markby, AN IDEAL HUSBAND, Belfast Lyric Theatre, George Roman

1991, Stage, Lady Kerrigan, TOVARICH, Chichester Festival Theatre &Triumph, Patrick Garland

Further Credits

Television, MINDER, Euston Films, Jim Hill

Television, THE GENTLE TOUCH, LWT, Nic Phillips

Television, LONDON'S BURNING, LWT, Gerry Mills & Gerry Poulson

Television, IT AIN'T HALF HOT MUM, BBC Television, David Croft

2004, Television, THE BILL, Thames Television

2004, Television, ABSOLUTE POWER, BBC Television

2003, Television, Various Roles, UNDER ONE ROOF, Prospect Films for ITV, Various Directors

1998, Television, Lisa, CASUALTY, BBC Television, Michael Owen Morris

1996, Video, Diane, CELLNET, Blue Print Productions, Derek Hanlon

1995, Television, Lady Weir, EMMERDALE, Yorkshire Television, Various

1994, Radio, Paulina, WINTERS TALE, BBC World Service, Gerard O'Malley

1994, Voice Over, READER'S DIGEST

1993, Television, Mrs. Lavers, NELSON'S COLUMN, BBC Television, Susie Belbin

Skills:

Accents & Dialects: American-California, American-New York, American-Southern States, Devon, East
(= native)* European, French, German*, Irish-Southern, London, Russian, Scottish-Standard, South African, Welsh-Standard

Languages: English*, French, German
(= mother tongue)*

Music & Dance: Aerobics, Ballet, Ballroom Dancing, Mezzo-Soprano, Period Dancing, Piano
(= highly skilled)*

Performance: Voice Over

Sports: Horse-jumping*, Horse-riding*, Swimming*
(= highly skilled)*

Vehicle Licences: Car Driving Licence

Other Skills: Computer Literate, Narration

■   a CV from an actor who doesn't have an agent:

Georgina Landau

Personal
m mobile number
e email address

Hair Brown ♦ **Eyes** Brown ♦ **Height** 5'8" ♦ **Nationality** British ♦ **Equity Status** Full
Training Mountview Academy of Theatre Arts BA(Hons) in Performance (Acting)

Theatre Experience

Role	Production	Director	Company
Sara	Romy and Julien	Sue Cosgrove	Vienna's English Theatre (International Tour)
Lisette	The Double Inconstancy	Michael Cabot	London Classic Theatre Clwyd Theatre Cymru (Tour)
Widow/Soldier	All's Well That Ends Well	Tim Sullivan	LOST Theatre
Lydia	Hunger	Rhiannon Jackson	Royal Court (Reading)
The Brunette	Bond Girls	Shane Morgan	Theatre West
Helena	The Error of Their Ways	Eleanor Rhode	Cockpit Theatre
Marie	Listed Lido	Tyne Rafaeli	Listed Theatre
Mabel	Before The Night Is Through	Suzy Catliff	Lucky Stuff Productions
Southern Lady/ French Maid	Lucky Stiff	Suzy Catliff	Lucky Stuff Productions
Rosetta	Leonce and Lena	Philip McGinley	Jam Factory Theatre Edinburgh Festival

Film, Television and Voice Experience

Office Worker	Boots 'Looking Good' Hayfever (Commercial)	Tony Barry	Academy Films/Mother
Jess Clark	The Burning Girl (Audio Book)	Tamsin Collinson	Time Warner Book Group UK
Tracey Bradley	A Northern Soul	Maxwell Thomas	Northern Film School
Faith	Commercial	Paul Williams	More 3
Claire	E's Up (Film)	Randhi McWilliams	N9 Media Zone

Mountview Experience

Isabella	Measure for Measure	Paul Clements	The Judi Dench Theatre
Constance	King John	Giles Smith	The Judi Dench Theatre
Laura	The Glass Menagerie	Georgia Bance	The Judi Dench Theatre
Innkeeper/Musician	The Caucasian Chalk Circle	Crispin Bonham-Carter	Chelsea Theatre
Edie	The American Clock	David Salter	The Greenwich Theatre

Skills

Singing	Mezzo-soprano (Grade 6)
Dance	Gold Medal Commended 19th/20th Century Social Dance (Merengue, Jive, Schottische, Tango, Waltz, Polka, Two Step Salsa, Mazurka & Charleston)
Instruments	Flute (Grade 4), Music Theory (Grade 5)
Accents	RP, General Northern, London, Welsh, West Country, French, German, General American, NY & Southern American. Excellent ear for accents
Sports	Tennis, Swimming
Other	Full clean driving license

■   CVs of actors direct from an agent:

JEREMY BROOK LIMITED

37 Berwick Street, London W1F 8RS
Tel: 020 7434 0398 Fax: 020 7287 8016
www.jeremybrookltd.co.uk
Email: info@jeremybrookltd.co.uk

BRYONY AFFERSON

Eyes BLUE-GREY	Height	5'5"
Hair RED	Training	East 15

TELEVISION

WALKING THE DOG	*Maid*	Sky Arts	Jeremy Brock
LUTHER	*Candida Calvert*	BBC 1	Sam Miller
THE SHADOW LINE (3 eps)	*Sara*	BBC 2	Hugo Blick
DOCTORS	*Alex Foreman*	BBC 1	Jim Larkin
LAW AND ORDER	*Alison*	Kudos for ITV 1	Andy Goddard
SURVIVORS	*Patricia*	BBC	John Alexander
THE BILL	*Ellie Rogers*	Talkback Thames	Nigel Douglas
WAKING THE DEAD (2 eps)	*Hunny*	BBC 1	Tim Fywell & Philippa Langdale
TOTALLY FRANK (2 series)	*Charlie*	Channel 4	Various

FILM

SOLD	*Amy*	Broco Media Films	Dave Cohen
AFRICAN GAME	*Kate*	Dania Film	Massimo Tarantini

THEATRE

A GOOD DEATH	*Sam*	N.T. Studio	Samantha Potter
ON THE WATERFRONT	*Edie Doyle*	Haymarket Theatre	Steven Berkoff
ROUGH MUSIC	*Jessie Sanders*	King's Head Theatre	John Adams
ON THE WATERFRONT	*Edie Doyle*	Three Mills Studios	Steven Berkoff

SKILLS
Accents: South Yorkshire (native), R.P, Glaswegian
Singing: Alto* F below middle C to top F
Instruments: Piano, Guitar*, Trumpet
Dance: Ballet, Tap, Jazz
Stage Combat BADC
Henry Cotton Award Winner 2003

*A Spotlight notation meaning highly skilled.

JEREMY BROOK LIMITED

37 Berwick Street, London W1F 8RS
Tel: 020 7434 0398 Fax: 020 7287 8016
www.jeremybrookltd.co.uk
Email: info@jeremybrookltd.co.uk

STUART BUNCE

Eyes	BLUE		Height	5'11"
Hair	DARK BROWN		Training	Guildhall

TELEVISION

RIPPER STREET	Preacher	BBC	Andy Wilson
CASUALTY	Franco	BBC	Robert Bierman
CLAPHAM JUNCTION	Gavin	Channel 4	Adrian Shergold
NUREMBERG –NAZIS ON TRIAL	Major Kelly	BBC	Mike Wadding
SPACE RACE	Gen. Gaidukov	BBC	Chris Spencer
EGYPT	J. J. Champollion	BBC	Ferdinand Fairfax
MURDER IN SUBURBIA	Ralph Mitchell	Carlton	Edward Bennet
SPARTACUS	Cornelius Lucas	ABC	Robert Dornhelm
INSPECTOR LYNLEY MYSTERIES	Damian Chambers	BBC	Brian Stirner
MIDSOMER MURDERS	Tony Parish	Carlton	Peter Smith
THE JURY	Charles Gore	Granada	Pete Travis
THE SCARLET PIMPERNEL	Phillipe Lispard	BBC	Graham Theakston
MRS BRADLEY MYSTERIES	Seth	BBC	Martin Hutchins
ALL THE KINGS MEN	Frederick Radley	BBC	Julian Jarrold
PEAK PRACTICE	Adam Prince	Granada	Terry McDonough
JEREMIAH	Baruch	Hallmark	Harry Winer
BABES IN THE WOOD	Ben	Carlton	Andy de Emmony
QUEENS PARK STORY	Gus	BBC	Barney Cokeliss
CASUALTY	Jeff	BBC	Dave Innes Edwards

FILM

FUTURE IMPERFECT	Simon	Fluidity Films	Roger Thorpe
THE GOSPEL OF JOHN	John	Visual Bible	Phillip Saville
THE LOST LOVER	Gabriel	Jean Vigo Italia	Roberto Faenza
REGENERATION	Wilfred Owen	BBC Films	Gillies McKinnon
FIRST KNIGHT	Peter	Columbia	Jerry Zucker
FATHERLAND	Blind Soldier	HBO	Chris Menaul
MAVIS DAVIS	Aspirant	BBC	John Henderson

THEATRE

THE SCHOOL FOR SCANDAL	Charles Surface	LA Theatre Works	Michael Hackett
CORIOLANUS	Coriolanus	Bloomsbury Theatre	Matthew Warchus
ROMEO & JULIET	Romeo	Lyric Hammersmith	Neil Bartlett
KING LEAR	Burgundy	RSC	Adrian Noble
PUSHKIN TRILOGY			
THE GOLDEN COCKEREL	Dadon	Edinburgh Festival	Anna Barkan
COUNT NULIN	Count Nulin	Edinburgh Festival	Anna Barkan
THE FEAST DURING THE PLAGUE	Chairman	Edinburgh Festival	Anna Barkan

RADIO / VOICE-OVER

THE BROWNING VERSION	Peter Gilbert	BBC Radio 4	Martin Jarvis
HOME TO THE BLACK SEA	Young Iskender	BBC Radio 4	Anastasia Tolstoy
HADJI MURAT	Captain Butler	BBC Radio 3	Marc Beeby
DOCUMENTARY NARRATION – 'The Hayley Oakines Story'		Channel 5	
DOCUMENTARY NARRATION – 'The Boy Who Lived Twice'		Channel 5	

SKILLS

Accents: American – Standard, East European, English – Standard*, Irish - Southern, London, RP, Russian, Scottish – Standard.

*A Spotlight notation meaning mother tongue.

You will also notice that there are different degrees, and types, of experience on each CV we have chosen.

It is very tempting to look at the photo on the CV, or see a list of credits, and make an instant judgement. But there are certain things you need to think about to make sure that the actors you choose to meet at a casting session are appropriate for the roles that you are seeing them for.

HOW TO READ A CV

I have to say reading a CV is an art that I didn't realise I had!

Tim Welton – director/producer

Take the time to read the CV carefully and consider the following factors:

Playing range

Remember it's not how old the actor actually is, but how old they *look* and how old they seem. A Spotlight photograph might be very flattering, or could be years out of date.

Playing range
The ages at which the actor can be believably cast.

If you are casting for stage or radio, a 25-year-old actress could play a 12-year-old, if their voice, physique and energy is right, but it is unlikely that you would make the same choice if casting for screen work because the audience is a lot closer and what might look like 12 on stage does not when magnified and on a screen.

Height

Beware of casting two actors who are very different heights if they have to play a lot of scenes together – unless you are making a point of that discrepancy. For screen, it makes it very difficult to frame a shot, whilst on stage it may not tell the story you intend.

Eye colour/colouring

Be aware of genetics when casting actors who are playing characters related to one another – two blue-eyed parents and a brown-eyed child won't work. Although, if everything else is right, and your budget allows, you could go for contact lenses. Also be aware of colouring when casting families – would two very dark-haired parents really have a natural blonde-haired, blue-eyed child? If you are casting from an ethnically diverse selection of actors, make sure that the whole creative team has agreed how different ethnicities affect the story you are telling.

Accent

If you are casting family members, as in the TV series *Shameless*, you will most likely be looking for actors who have the same accent – or who can do the same accent – in order to make it believable and truthful. Actors' CVs should list their native accents and those that they can speak convincingly.

Ensemble

Ensemble
A script where there is no specific 'lead' character but instead a group of characters all of whom develop and share the narrative.

If you are casting an **ensemble** – for example, a group of friends who are all around the same age and background, as in the TV series *Skins* – you need to look for actors who complement or contrast each other.

Once you've identified whether the actor looks and sounds right, go to the body of the CV where the actor will have listed the work they have done. What should you be looking for there?

☐   Using your personal knowledge

Read the list of work the actor has done. Have you seen any of it? Did you like it?

☐   What type of work have they done?

Take note of whether it is mostly amateur or college productions. You need to know that the actor has the appropriate experience for the role you are casting. If you are about to do a long rehearsal period for an experimental drama, then someone with experience in only short films might not be the right choice for your needs.

☐   What medium are they most experienced in?

There are many actors who work across screen and stage regularly and successfully. But, some stage actors' qualities never really transmit to screen and vice versa. Take this into consideration when reading the credits on an actor's CV.

☐   What directors have they worked with?

This will give you an idea about the actor, their tastes, and how other practitioners have cast them. Also note whether an actor has worked for the same director on more than one occasion, as this can indicate that they are capable of forming a good working relationship.

SHOWREELS

The physical things are really important – even if they've only got a tiny showreel of stuff they've done themselves – or a voice tape – that's really useful, because you start to put together a three dimensional view of that person.

Tim Welton – director/producer

Most actors have a showreel with selections from their screen work, which will be included on the actor's Spotlight page, or there will be a link that you can follow. By watching their showreel, you will get an idea of how they look and sound, and it will definitely help you to decide whether to meet the actor for the role you had in mind.

But, don't judge solely from the show reel. Use it as a tool and make sure you meet the actor in person.

Don't discount an actor who looks interesting, but hasn't got a showreel. If they have the right experience, qualities and fulfil your other criteria, it is always worth meeting them.

WHICH ROLE TO CAST FIRST?

You've got to have your lynchpin, there's always one person that you've got to build around.

Kate Rhodes James – casting director

Whilst you have been doing your research on the script, there may be one part which is the obvious lead. For example, in a conventional production of Shakespeare's Hamlet, Hamlet would be the pivotal role. However, there may be a role which you have decided is key to your concept. For example, in Shakespeare's *Othello*, the character of Iago, rather than the character of Othello, might be central to your vision. Perhaps there is an energy and chemistry which is vital, as in the casting of Bella and Edward in the *Twilight* trilogy.

WHO TO SEE?

You have decided on the pivotal role, or roles, and you have read the CVs thoroughly. Now you are ready to make a list of the actors you want to meet.

Here is an example of a list we have drawn up for a casting of Iago and Othello.

CHARACTER	ACTOR NAME	CONTACT INFORMATION	REASONS FOR SEEING
Iago	Joe Bloggs	000-0000	Very fit and athletic. Right playing age. Intelligent eyes. Lots of stage experience but no Shakespeare.
Othello	Jim Bloggs	222-2222	Very imposing. Nigerian with a lot of classical experience. Black belt in karate.
Othello	Jay Bloggs	Agent – XXXX	More classical theatre on his CV, maybe a bit older than we were thinking, but worth a meet.
Iago	Josh Bloggs	Agent – XXXX	Saw him on TV and also in a fringe musical – really interesting energy and intensity.

■ **Exercise 7 – deciding who to see**

If there are both a producer and director working on the production, then they should go through the CVs and showreels separately and draw up their own lists. Here is a template for you to fill in for your production.

CHARACTER	ACTOR NAME	CONTACT INFORMATION	REASONS FOR SEEING

PLANNING THE SESSION

Now you know who you want to meet for the different roles, you need to make some decisions about what you are going to do during the session.

The casting session is as much a part of your project as the production itself, so you need to give it the same care and attention.

In the industry, casting sessions vary, according to the way a director and producer like to work, on the size of the production, where the production is based and the type of media: theatre, TV or film. Casting directors are responsible for setting up the casting sessions in commercial theatre, film and TV, whilst in regional and subsidised theatre the director's team will usually organize the session. Radio often takes the form of a telephone audition.

What sort of session and what to do in it?

A chat about the role – You might be very interested in an actor whose work you have seen, but you would like to meet them before offering them a role. This is perfectly acceptable. You need to prepare the questions you would like to ask them so that you can find out about their take on the role, the script and the production.

If you go for this type of meeting, prepare some questions you want to ask them to get a sense of whether you feel they are right for the part

A chat (with reading) – This type of meeting will consist of a chat to get to know the actor and the actor being asked to read from the script. This is the usual format for both theatre and film auditions.

Reading
Hearing a scene read out loud.

It is useful to ask the actors you are auditioning to learn or prepare a speech or a scene from the script. If the scene includes dialogue with another character/s then be sure you agree with your team who is going to be reading the other roles. If you have a casting director on board, then they will read the dialogue with the actor, to allow the director and producer to focus on the actor and their interpretation.

A workshop – This is more appropriate if you are casting a family, a group of friends, or putting together a company of actors for a devised piece. You need to find out whether your actors go together, whether the chemistry is right, whether they complement one another and whether they will create the dynamic you are looking for. In these instances a group audition or workshop is a good idea. You will need to ensure you have the right space and that you have planned the session to allow you to observe and note each of the actors.

Be sure to inform the actors that this is the type of session they are attending.

Exercises to use in a group workshop audition

'Getting to know you' exercises for the group.

Remember, it is probable that none of the group will know each other and in order to get the best out of them, and see how they work together, it is worthwhile spending a little time getting them to relax with each other.

Here are some ideas to start you off on a workshop but there are plenty of books you can find that have excellent games and exercises you can try. We have suggested a few classics below.

As with everything, you will need to practice to become confident, so don't worry if it takes a few goes to get concentration going and to get the games working properly. If you are running the workshop, be clear and concise about your directions and be prepared to take the lead – literally.

☐   EXERCISE 1: Information exchange

Objectives: to relax the group; to have a bit of fun; to get them to know at least one other person a little better; and for each member of the group to get to know some information about the other group members.

Practical: Pair them up and ask them to find out five interesting things about the other person – excluding their name, which is a given.

Give them approximately three to five minutes to do this.

Then ask them to tell the whole group the facts about the other person that they have been working with.

☐ EXERCISE 2: Who is leading?

Objectives: to see how well they work together without verbal communication/how they communicate silently and how good their concentration and focus is.

Practical: Ask one group member to stand in a corner of the room with their eyes closed and back turned to the group. Ask the rest of the group to stand in a circle. Silently point to one of the group in the circle and ask them to start an action (i.e. head nodding/arm shaking/foot tapping) which the rest of the group then copies. Then ask the outside group member to stand in the centre of the circle and try and guess 'who is leading'? The person chosen to lead needs to change the action every 30 seconds or so. The person in the middle has three chances to guess.

☐ EXERCISE 3: Sheriff

Objectives: To gauge concentration and focus and how well they respond. This should be a high energy game and great fun – it may take some time to get going. It is also known as 'Bang'.

Practical: Assign yourself or one of the group to be the 'sheriff' which means you stand in the middle of the circle and point at one of the group on the outer circle, shouting 'bang' as you do so. That person ducks (to avoid your shot) and the people on either side of them turn and point and shout 'bang'. The person who is slowest at shooting or ducking is out and has to sit down – but still stay in their place within the circle.

Remember: It all depends on how you are approaching your work and what you want from the actors. Most actors enjoy playing games but not all do. However, if you are putting together an ensemble then it is imperative to find out how the group works together and it is highly unlikely that an actor who doesn't like participating with other actors in this way is going to be the right person for your project.

After the warm up games:

You may have sent the actors the script beforehand and asked them to look at a certain character – now is the time to put some pairings or groups together and see how they work/look.

You could split them into groups/pairs and ask them to work on a section of the piece to present back to the group or to be filmed.

You could pick out a theme or motif from the script and ask them to work in groups to bring you back an improvised scene. In this way you can observe how the different personalities work together in a group situation and who seems to be leading/hanging back.

Suggested further reading
The Improvisation Game: Discovering the Secrets of Spontaneous Performance by Chris Johnston (2006): Nick Hern Books, London, UK

100+ Ideas for Drama by Anna Scher and Charles Verrall (1975): Heinemann, UK

Theatre Games for Young Performers by Maria C. Novelly (1991): Meriwether Publishing, Colorado Springs, US

Pages
Selection of scenes from a script sent to actors prior to a meeting.

Preparing pages
If you are going to ask an actor to read from the script, you must send the script to them in advance.

Audition Speech
Most actors, particularly those fresh from training, will have two or three monologues in their repertoire to show off their acting skills.

If you would like the actor to do a monologue at the meeting, then include this information in the breakdown. The actor needs time to prepare.

Improvisation
Spontaneously reacting to stimuli that may or may not be script based.

Improvisation
Improvisation is a skill and it can be a useful tool, if a director knows how it works and why they want to use it. Actors may have been trained, or have experience, in improvisation but it is not something an actor can just launch into and it won't inform you in the casting process without a clear understanding of why you are doing it and what you hope to learn. If you do plan to use improvisation in the session, make it clear in the breakdown.

Which scenes to choose

■ Lead roles

In order to know if the actor is able to find the beats or the tone of the script, *you* need to know it inside out. The scenes that you choose should be fundamental to your vision of the piece. Choose them carefully and for a reason. It is always best to choose scenes that demonstrate:

- key moments in the character's story arc

- relationship high points – so that you can explore the possibilities of the scene with the actor and the emotional core of the character

- a significant turning point for the character.

You should, as a matter of course, send the whole script to the actor, to allow them to contextualize their role. If asking them to prepare specific scenes, make sure they know the page/scene numbers that you will be working on.

- Supporting roles

> *Sometimes very small character parts are vital. The third character on the left for one scene is important – because if they get the scene wrong, and don't make an impression, the scene is lost.*
>
> Tim Bradley – TV producer

If you are casting a character who only speaks in one scene, or even has no lines at all, what should you do in the session?

- if they have any dialogue at all, you should use that scene

- ask the actor to prepare something for the meeting such as a character back story

- film them as they chat with you – as long as you have asked their permission beforehand.

> *If you get it cast right, then it works. I can't overestimate how much a good actor, in the right role, brings.*
>
> John Griffin – executive producer

Case Study – the artistic director

Joe Sumsion is Artistic Director of a regional theatre in Lancashire, producing high quality work that is relevant to the community thus ensuring that the theatre remains an integral part of that community.

JS: I was born and brought up in Kendal – 25 miles north of Lancaster. I got my Equity card here at The Dukes Playhouse as an assistant stage manager when I was 19 and now I am Director.

Q: How's that been? Running a theatre?

JS: It's fantastic in the main, because you've got lots of opportunities to make great work. The Dukes isn't just a theatre, it's a cultural centre for Lancaster and Lancashire so you can help other people realise their creative ambitions, and that's the bit I find the most exciting about it.

Q: How many home grown productions do you do a year and at what stage do you begin to think about casting?

JS: For the past few years, it's been five a year. We often cast people we know, people we've worked with before and sometimes those people are cast ahead of a more open casting process. For example, the Christmas show we've got on at the moment has a cast of six, and one of those people was cast last February because she was in the Christmas show last year and she was great and she had some particular skills that we knew we were after. But the others were cast in an open application process and we did interviews in September. We start thinking about it when the play is programmed – say a year in advance – but the main bulk of the casting takes place about three months before we go into the rehearsals.

Q: How important would you say that casting is to the project?

JS: Well, I've got a mate who's a composer and he says, 'casting and booking of creative teams is 80 per cent of the director's job' – I do think it is the most important thing you do and if you get a good cast working on a good script, you're almost bound to succeed – whereas if you get a problematic cast, however much work you put in – you're almost bound to fail.

Q: Do you think over the years you've got better at it?

JS: Yes, I think you get better at understanding actors' technical abilities but also better at judging what people are really like – not as actors but as people – we try to cast really talented people and at the same time try to cast people who are going to be a good team. The person we don't want is the exceptionally talented actor who is a pain for the company. A team is paramount.

Q: How would you say you look for that? How do you audition?

JS: We always allow at least 20 minutes per actor and it's always worth seeing if people have a good sense of humour – a bit like those dating columns that say 'good sense of humour' required – in a funny way, casting is a bit like that. Sometimes we do workshop auditions – we see people individually for 15 minutes and then at the end of the morning do a workshop with about eight, and you really get a feel for people and how they interact.

Q: Do you work with a casting director?

JS: No, a lot of the work we do here is new writing, so the writer is often involved. Jackie Wilson, who is the theatre secretary, co-ordinates casting – she's been here for a long time and knows a lot of the people who have worked here before and often has good suggestions. And the composer or musical director – that person would always be at the auditions anyway, if there's a musical element to it. Those are the people you generally talk to.

Q: So, when you write a breakdown, what's important?

JS: Age, details of the role, and any particular things such as a particular accent – about a year ago we did a play set amongst the Polish community and authentic Polish accents were very important. So, things that are very specific to the play, but also key elements of character. For the Polish play, one particular actress that we found was of Romanian origin and her quality was not specifically Polish, but she had an aura about her which was very interesting to watch and connected particularly well with this particular part. The writer of that play, who is part Polish herself played an important role in casting the production.

Q: If it's a new piece, do you get them to read it?

JS: Yes, we always send a script. And have the writer involved in the audition process, as it's another way of finding out about the play and gives the actors a good idea of what the process is going to be like, and how the writer is going to be involved in rehearsals. We always read from the script, sometimes we ask people to do their own pieces and sometimes we do a workshop audition. I always ask people what they think of the script – you can learn a lot about people from that.

Q: About their personality and character?

JS: Yes, and a kind of theatrical understanding. For me, the best actors kind of understand how plays work, as well as understand how to present a character. With new work you always have to look after the story so you want to work with actors who understand narrative, because that's going to affect the choices they make and how they play the parts.

CHAPTER 6

SETTING UP THE SESSION

- ■ Arranging the meeting
- ■ Organizing your session
- ■ The logistics of the session
- ☐ Case study – the TV series producer

■ SETTING UP THE SESSION

You are putting together a visual story. A visual story of the play.
Nadine Rennie – casting director

You have decided upon the actors you would like to meet and the way in which you are going to run your casting session. The next step is organization.

ARRANGING THE MEETING

You will need to contact the actors' agents, if they have one, or contact the actors direct with all the details of the meeting. You will need to tell them:

■ the venue
■ the time
■ who they will be meeting
■ what will be expected of them at the meeting – i.e. will they be reading from a script, improvising, working with other actors, recorded or put on tape.

If an agent or actor has sent their CV following receipt of your breakdown, it should mean that they are available for your dates. However, it is always wise to check their availability again, when you arrange the time to meet them. (See Chapter 3 for further information regarding availability checks.)

ORGANIZING YOUR SESSION

Ensure that you keep careful records of the names of actors, the roles you are seeing them for, the contact details of their agent and what pages you have asked them to prepare.

Below is an example of a method of organizing your session. Be sure to keep it up to date, so that you know who you are seeing and when you are seeing them, and if anyone changes an appointment.

Meeting organization

NAME	BEING SEEN FOR	AGENT/CONTACT DETAILS	AVAILABILITY	MEETING DATE/ TIME	PAGES SENT

THE LOGISTICS OF THE SESSION

Who is going to be in the session?

Decide who is going to be in the session, so that you can inform the agent or actor in advance. Be sure everyone is there for a reason. The director definitely needs to be there to find out if they can work with the actor. The producer should be there and possibly the writer, if it is a new piece and is appropriate. We suggest that you have at least two people in the room because:

■ it is useful to have someone else to bounce ideas off

■ it makes the whole process easier and more enjoyable

■ it shares responsibility

■ they can keep an eye on timings allowing the director to focus on the actor

■ they can help keep the conversation going if things get stuck.

You need to have decided the following prior to the casting session:

■ who is going to be the 'meeter and greeter'?

■ who is going to lead the meeting?

■ who is going to talk about the project?

■ who is going to ask about the actor's previous work?

■ who is going to read from the script?

■ who is going to operate the camera (if you need one)?

Use the template below to organize who is going to do what.

Who does what at the audition

TASK	NAME	PREPARE
Meet and greet		
Lead the meeting		
Talk about the project		
Talk about the CV		
Read in with the actor		
Camera operation		

Even if there are only two of you in the meeting, it is always best to decide upon who is doing what so that you don't miss covering anything vital. However, we would suggest a maximum of four people in the meeting, otherwise you could overwhelm the actor.

Being this organized is really important – just as you are choosing your actors based on their performance, so the actors will be judging *your* professionalism and organizational skills.

Where to do the session?

Where you do your casting session will depend on what your project is, what you want to do during the session and your budget. Essentially, you need to ensure the space you arrange is appropriate and comfortable.

For a chat with reading – you will need enough space for a table and chairs for everyone at the session and possibly space for a camera to be set up, so that you can record the actor. It can be a meeting room, a classroom, a front room – just make sure it is clean and comfortable.

For a workshop – find a space that is flexible – somewhere to sit and talk about what you are going to do, which can then be cleared for the actors to move about. It doesn't have to be a big studio, just a clear and clean space where you will be uninterrupted.

What do you want from the session?

To find out if the actors you are meeting have the range, skills and qualities necessary. Do you believe in that actor as the character? Could you work together creatively? How do you find out?

■ talk to them, explain your ideas for the script and the character, your vision for the piece. And listen to their ideas and thoughts

■ work on their interpretation of the character.

To film or not to film?

If your production is for the screen, then it is appropriate to record the actor to see how their performance and persona comes across when recorded.

For a theatre audition, or any kind of live production, recording the actor is not necessary because the qualities you are looking for are not necessarily going to be successfully captured.

If you *are* going to film the auditions, make sure you know how to work the camera, and where to position it.

> *They can be great in the room but then give yourself a few days gap and review them. It's really important.*
>
> Kate Rhodes James – casting director

How much time for each actor?

> *I think about 25 minutes is a good time for a theatre meeting.*
>
> Nadine Rennie – casting director

It is important not to rush the meeting. Never underestimate the time needed to 'get your eye in' – the first actor you meet will inevitably be a bit of a shock, as it is often the first time that you have heard the part read by an actor. So allow for this when working out your timings. It is always much better to allow more time for the first couple of actors that you are meeting.

Be realistic and generous about how much time to give each actor. 15 to 20 minutes is a good average. If you are seeing an actor for a major lead role you should allow longer: long enough to tell them about the project, give them time to relax, talk a bit about themselves and the work they have done, giving *you* time to get to know them a little. You will begin to see if they are someone you could imagine working with. You should also leave enough time to hear them read.

Here is a timings sheet that we have completed using the casting of Romeo, Juliet, Paris and the Friar from *Romeo and Juliet* as an example of how to allocate appropriate times. We have allowed half an hour for Romeo and Juliet and 15 minutes for the Friar and Paris.

Audition Timings example

TITLE OF PROJECT: Romeo and Juliet

VENUE OF CASTING SESSION: Room 207, Queen's
                                      Youth Club

DATE/TIME OF CASTING SESSION: Monday, 27th June

NAMES OF DIRECTOR/PRODUCER: Jane Smith/John Doe

CONTACT NUMBERS: xxx xxxxx/xxx xxxxx

10.00   Team to meet in room.
                                      Room and camera set up

TIME*	NAME	ROLE NAME	AGENT/CONTACT
10.10	Actor 1	Paris	Agent name
10.25	Actor 2	Juliet	Agent name
10.55	Actor 3	Friar	Agent name
11.10	Actor 4	Romeo	Agent name
11.40	Actor 5	Paris	Agent name
11.55	Actor 6	Friar	Agent name
12.10	Actor 7	Juliet	Agent name
12.40	Re-cap/discussion		
1.00	Session finishes		

*This gives 30 minutes per lead role, i.e. Romeo and Juliet, and 15 minutes per supporting role.

Audition Timings

TITLE OF PROJECT:

VENUE OF CASTING SESSION:

DATE/TIME OF CASTING SESSION:

NAMES OF DIRECTOR/PRODUCER:

CONTACT NUMBERS:

Team to meet in room.
Room and camera set up

TIME*	NAME	ROLE	AGENT/CONTACT
	Re-cap/discussion		
	Session finishes		

*Remember to give 30 minutes per lead and 15 minutes per supporting role.

Allow yourself enough time for each actor, and keep to your schedule, so that you don't become stressed and end up seeing actors too quickly, not giving yourself a chance to find out whether they are right for your production.

From the actor's point of view, they need you to run on schedule, as they could have other meetings or a job that they need to get to. If they are anxious because you are running late, they won't give a good audition. As you become more experienced and confident – or are able to employ a casting director – your timings will become more accurate.

Try not to see too many actors at one session. It will be exhausting if you are giving each actor the same amount of time and attention.

I was in New York years ago with the friend of mine who was a casting director and she was auditioning for a show where they had to be able to act, sing and skateboard. I said "How long are the auditions?" and she said "Oh well, it's legislated by the Equity rules in New York, the minimum length of the audition," and I said "What's that?" Guess what it was? The minimum length of the audition? 40 seconds! They were seeing people for 40 seconds and then threw them out. A whole gang of people were seeing them.

Mike Leigh – director

Case Study – the tv series producer

John Griffin *has sat both sides of the table – he had a career as a jobbing actor for 20 years before starting work in TV as a script editor, and working his way up to producing some of the most current cutting edge contemporary drama.*

JG: It's vital to get the casting right. Particularly a new cast of something – if you get it cast right, then it works. I can't overestimate how much a good actor, in the right role, brings.

A really good example is on the second generation of *Skins* – we had a character called Cook, who nobody liked on the page and we worried terribly about him because we said nobody's going to like him – why are we writing such an unsympathetic character right at the centre of the show? Then after having done a lot of work to try and redeem this character, we cast Jack O'Connell, and I saw about five minutes of him on rushes and went, 'Oh, we're fine!' Because he's brilliant and, actually, I find him absolutely captivating. He just got it and has charisma and, although I don't like him, I've got to see more of him.

Sometimes, everybody's disagreeing, or nobody quite gets the part, or we don't quite know what we're looking for so we can't find it. In *Shameless*, we wanted an older guy to be Carol's boyfriend who was a nudist – and they all came in and it was like watching *Last of the Summer Wine* – they were all thinking 'It's *Shameless*, it's funny – I'll do comedy acting' it was like no, no, no, this person has got to take it completely seriously. And then we found Paul Copley, who was just *brilliant*. And he's another one, I just go, 'Oh god, he saved us!'

He said 'I refused to come to the audition the first time because I knew I had to take my clothes off and I didn't want to – and then they sent the script and I read it and thought 'Damn, it's a really good part'." And then he said 'Mind you, it does say he's well endowed in the script – should I warn you?'

One of the greatest joys of working in series television is writing to what you're watching – so as soon as there's any assembly of first episodes with the character in, you're watching them to see what they're giving you, and then you start writing to their strengths very, very quickly because that's how they're going to look best.

For example, by far the best way of writing a new character in a show like *Shameless* is to develop one who has been in the series at some point in the past and we've just liked them. By the third series of *Shameless*, it was just a kind of rolling casting going on of characters for episodes and occasionally new characters.

And Mickey McGuire had come in for one episode for a gag part – he was going to fall in love with Ian, and he was just so brilliant that we went 'We've got to get him in'. We had to scrabble around finding money in the budget, you know, to keep him in episodes during the series he was in – that he hadn't been storylined for – ready for the next series when he was written in from the start.

CHAPTER 7

THE SESSION PART 1

- ■ Setting up
- ■ Pre-casting checklist
- ■ Meeting and greeting
- ☐ Case study – the fringe actor

■ THE SESSION PART 1

You've done your research, put in the time looking for the right actors, checked their availability and interest, booked a meeting place, given the actors and their agents a time to meet and sent them pages to prepare.

You are now ready for the most important part of the process – meeting the actors who will become your flesh and blood characters and bring the script to life. This is the exciting moment when you find out whether they embody what you envision, surprise and excite you.

This chapter takes you from the moment you arrive at your audition venue to the moment your first actor walks into the room.

I give the actor masses of information, everything they need to know about the production and the part. I create a character breakdown that is a snapshot of who the character is and get the material to them before the day so there is no awful sight reading panic.

Marina Caldarone – director

SETTING UP

Get to the audition venue early and allow yourself enough time before the first actors arrive to prepare.

☐ Outside the room:

■ Put notices on doors so that anyone arriving is clear where they should go and where they should wait.
■ If at all possible, ensure the actors wait in a separate area from the audition, so they cannot overhear. There is nothing more disconcerting and unsettling than hearing another actor reading the same part that you are about to go in for.
■ If you have information that you want the actors to read about your production, lay it out in the waiting area.

☐ Inside the room:

■ Arrange tables and chairs for everyone who is going to be in the session.
■ Ensure the chair that the actor will sit on is situated so that they can make eye contact with everyone.

■ Clear away tables and chairs if the audition is going to take the form of a workshop.

■ Organize all the CVs of the actors and make sure that everyone in the session has copies. However, make sure the *actors* can't see the CVs of the other actors who you are meeting.

□ Preparation:

■ Everyone will need something to make notes on.

■ Turn off your mobile phones.

■ If you are using a camera to record the session, test the power, (ensure there is space on the card), lighting, sound and framing for the actor's position.

■ Have enough copies of the script so that everyone in the room has one and you have a spare if an actor needs it.

Personnel:

■ Ensure meeter and greeter has a phone so that agents or actors can call if they are delayed or lost.

■ Whatever you decide to do, make sure you all know the plan and present a professional and supportive front to the actor.

■ Everyone needs a copy of the timings sheet so that you can all keep an eye on the schedule and run the meeting on time.

Pre-casting session checklist – make sure you have checked all these boxes.

TO DO	CHECK
Put notices on the doors with clear arrows directing actors where to go.	
Try to position the waiting area out of earshot of the audition.	
Lay out printed information about your production or company for actors to read.	
Arrange tables and chairs for the team who will be in the room.	
Ensure the actor will be able to make eye contact with everyone from their chair.	
Clear away extra tables and chairs if you are running a workshop audition.	
Organize CVs of all the actors you are going to see and ensure all those in the session have a copy.	
Ensure everyone in the room has something to make notes on.	
Test the camera – ensure the sound is working – and check framing.	
Have spare copies of the pages/script so that everyone in the room has a copy and ensure there are enough spares for actors if they have forgotten theirs.	
Ensure meeter and greeter has a phone and the numbers of the actors and agents.	
Ensure everyone in the session has a copy of the timings sheet.	

MEETING AND GREETING

Try and chat - they are nervous. I would be nervous, they don't know who they're meeting... introduce yourself properly... be helpful, so when they start they know who's there.

Beryl Vertue – producer, Hartswood Films

Remember that by being there in person, the actor has already shown an interest in your project and the role they are being seen for. The casting session is also for the actor to find out whether they want to work with *you* and whether they feel it will be a creative and enjoyable experience. It is an interview on both sides. This is true whether or not a fee is involved. If an actor is going to give their time and energy, it is important that they know they are in safe hands and that it is going to be a worthwhile experience.

Whatever kind of session you are going to run, there are a few notes on how to behave that will make all the difference to how comfortable an actor feels, and consequently, how well they come across.

☐ Do:

- stand up when the actor comes into the room
- introduce yourself and your team
- be friendly and interested
- have some small talk prepared – where they have come from/how was their journey?

☐ Do not:

- text or email at any time whilst an actor is in the room
- look bored or disappointed when they arrive
- be silent or mumble.

Have a look at the script below as an example of good practice.

```
INT. A ROOM. DAY

There are a few chairs in a rough semi-circle, with a chair
in front, facing them. There is a table in the corner with a
selection of scenes and scripts on it.

Seated on two of the chairs are the DIRECTOR and the
PRODUCER. They are looking through the CV's of the actors
they are about to see. The door opens.

THE MEETER & GREETER enters with ACTOR.  As they come into
the room, the DIRECTOR and PRODUCER stand up and look
interested - because they are!

                    MEETER & GREETER
          Hello, this is (insert Actor's
          name).

The Director shakes the Actor's hand.

                    DIRECTOR
          Hi, I'm (insert director's name) -
          pleased to meet you.

                    ACTOR
          Hi - pleased to meet you.
```

```
                        PRODUCER
          Hi there. I'm (insert producer's
          name). Thanks for coming in.

S/he points to the chair in the middle of the room. The
Meeter&Greeter leaves the room.

                        PRODUCER (CONT'D)
          Please do take a seat.

Everyone sits - the Director and Producer opposite the Actor.

                        DIRECTOR
          So, have you had a chance to look
          at the script?

                        ACTOR
          Yes, I thought it was great.

                        PRODUCER
          We really enjoyed seeing you in
          (insert name of play/tv/film)

The Actor is flattered and pleased.

                        ACTOR
          Oh! Thank you. Yes, it was great, I
          found the character very.....

AND WE ARE UP AND RUNNING.
```

I think good casting is absolutely about bringing together people who will work well together.

Vincent Franklin – actor

Actors don't just rely on their agents to find and put them up for work, they are constantly on the look out for work that sounds interesting, that will give them a worthwhile creative experience, allow them to collaborate and flex their acting muscles. They will follow up leads from the casting websites and once committed to a project will be a true professional and remain with it to the – sometimes bitter – end.

It is up to you – as the director and/or producer, even if there is no money changing hands, to act equally professionally. Read Sasha Morphitis' cautionary story.

Case Study – the fringe actor

Sasha trained as an actor at Mountview Academy of Theatre Arts, graduating with a BA (Hons) in Musical Theatre.

SM: I was represented at the time but it had nothing to do with my agent – I read about it in PCR and went for an audition. It said it was a tour, an adaptation of a poem by T.S. Eliot. At the audition they explained that it was expenses only and they got me to read some poetry and then put it into a kind of physical something – to be honest, I don't know what he wanted! But I basically went with it and it was probably one of the most surreal auditions because I remember at some point writhing about on the floor whilst the director said it was a passion project of his.

It was a three woman show – and at the audition he said that there would be, well, not *nudity* exactly but 'kind of like, you know' – he asked how would we feel about being scantily clad, (he didn't actually say 'scantily clad'). We were going to be painted as white statues so it wasn't going to be realistic to be wearing full clothes – and I said that was fine.

We rehearsed day times for three weeks – in a guide hut in Ruislip – so we all had to take time off work to be there. The first day he didn't show up because the producer – who turned out to be his ex-girlfriend – her dog had had puppies so they couldn't be there. So I'd taken a day off work to turn up to rehearsals and they didn't show up. This is how it all began. The other two actors were lovely women but he would argue if we made suggestions – and yet he'd said it would be a workshop environment where we would all experiment by testing the water. You have to know why you're doing it and how you're going to go about doing it. And he didn't.

When I realised that, I probably should have said, 'Thank you very much for the opportunity, but no thank you.' But I didn't because I thought it's not professional to turn work down once you've agreed to it. When we had one week of rehearsals left, the director had an argument with the French actress about being scantily clad on stage, he fired her on the pretext that her accent was too strong – which I thought was absolutely appalling as she'd auditioned with the same accent and he hadn't had a problem with it then.

He then relied on us to find someone to replace her – I roped in a very good, versatile actress friend of mine in the end, because otherwise I felt we would have just wasted two weeks of our time. Laura (*the friend*) then learned the whole part in one week.

So we got to performance and we thought that we'd have body paint but, because there was no budget, he got children's poster paint, which isn't made for skin. It was winter, in small theatres with not much heating and we'd spend an hour or so before going on stage slathering ourselves with this white paint – which was freezing cold. I can't believe now that we actually did it. I remember in one theatre – I think it was the Camden theatre – it was a tiny area backstage and there was a show before ours and they had loads of people in their cast. The dressing room was miniscule and you could only fit two people in it, and we were getting ready in a corridor with windows open and slathering paint on and actually shivering.

And basically once the paint dried, you couldn't really move very much because it would all start to crack off. Poster paint doesn't work like body paint in the slightest, because when it dries it just goes hard – so you're basically in a shell, kind of walking around like a mummy like this *(puts hands out)*. The idea was that we'd crack out of our statues so by the end of the hour performance, we were pretty much naked because all the poster paint had cracked off us.

Part of the piece was to throw a bucket of blue wet poster paint over our heads at the end! I think it was supposed to represent the Hindu god, Shiva, with all the arms and we passed the bucket and we had to get ourselves all covered in paint. This was the director's idea; we were not happy about it but, like everything else in the production so far, we just went along with it.

Q: Were you wearing underwear or bikinis?

SM: Tiny underwear. So by this point our relationship was frayed. We paid our own train fare to get to Leicester and Birmingham and he still owed us that money. Plus he said he'd put us up in accommodation but we slept on a mattress on the floor in his friend's student house – three of us on one mattress on the floor of somebody else's living room. And the thing is we were all quite happy-go-lucky about it. This is what you do with fringe stuff. We knew what we got ourselves into in the beginning. But actually looking back, I don't think we did agree to all that.

He presented himself at the audition as knowing what he was talking about. He sat behind the desk, and explained that he didn't have the money, but then he didn't say, 'You're going to have poster paint on your body.' He didn't tell us these things beforehand – he wasn't honest. He just didn't have a clue what he was doing.

At the end we said, 'We're not going on stage, unless you give us the money you owe us', and he got really offended and paid us the money but he pulled the last three nights of the show. I mean it hadn't sold well but why would you do that? But then at the end of the day, 'We aren't earning any money, we're cold, we're miserable, we're covered in blue paint – your loss.'

It was a farce and anyone else could see that – including us – and we did our utmost best to be professional and take it very seriously and do our best with something that had been broken from the start. He still thought it was still brilliant, a work of art: 'What's the fuss? Just put your poster paint on and get on with it!'

CHAPTER 8

THE SESSION PART 2

- ■ The chat
- ■ The read
- ■ How to bring the meeting to a close
- ☐ Case study – the head of casting

■ THE SESSION PART 2

This chapter takes you through how to talk to the actor and get the best out of them.

When meeting actors for a casting session you need to be open, receptive and pleased to see them. You want them to see you at your best so that they can be at their best too.

Every actor goes in and tries to do a really great job.

Ruby Snape – actor

THE CHAT

Actors are at the best when they feel relaxed

Damien Goodwin – director

Making conversation

Start with general topics of conversation – such as their journey in to meet you, where they live or even the weather. Breaking the ice and being relaxed is a vital part of the process.

When you are preparing for the meeting and re-reading each actor's CV, find a couple of questions to ask them about their previous work. If you have seen them onstage or in a film or television programme, this is an ideal starting point.

☐ Do:

■ congratulate them on their latest performance – which you saw and enjoyed
■ ask them which recent job they have enjoyed most
■ ask them about a specific recent job listed on their CV and what they enjoyed about it
■ ask them what was their favourite role.

☐ Do not:

■ admit you've never seen them in anything
■ admit you have seen them in something but hated it
■ ask them if they are working at the moment/have been working recently (everyone can be sensitive on this point) – be assured if they do have acting work at the moment, they will tell you about it

- tell them you haven't read their CV
- comment that their photo doesn't look anything like them, or that they look older than their photo. Saying that they look younger than their photo isn't usually a major faux pas!

Talking about the project
Discuss your ideas, vision and thoughts about the production. The more passionate and committed you are to your project, the more likely the actor is to become excited by the whole idea as well.

Asking the actor to read
Now is the time to ask the actor to present what they have prepared or show a particular skill that you are auditioning for.

For example, an actor needs a wide range of skills for a musical theatre job. We talked to David Grindrod, casting director for many West End and touring musicals, about his audition process:

> DG: The first stage is the actor comes in and sings and you think they could be that character... so you start to put your pile together. And then they come back to do a movement or dance call, and then a script call and then music – they come back four to five times – but each time it's more specific and you hone it right down. And then, once you know they have the skills, it comes down to the look – do you want all your blind mice the same size or do you want two tall and a short, or do you want big girls or do you want smaller.

Order of meeting
It is entirely up to you whether or not you want to start with work on the script or by having a general chat – the important thing is to have a plan.

Our view is that, as actors generally need time to warm-up, the chat is a great way to help them feel comfortable and confident.

Stay flexible – if you find, for example, that you are over running your time slot because of reading all the scenes the actor has prepared, then you don't need to hear every single scene; or you find that talking to them about the character is far more useful than reading – change the format of the meeting. Remember, the aim of the meeting is to find out as much as possible about the actor and whether they are right for your project, not to adhere rigidly to a format.

THE READ

Now we move on to the script itself and asking the actor to read the pages they have prepared.

You need to know why you have chosen the specific scenes to work on and what you would like the actor to find in the scenes. This is part of your preparation work ahead of the casting.

Consider the following, when looking at scenes:

- What is the feel?
  Is your project a farce, a black comedy or a thriller? Use a scene that allows the actor to show their skills in a specific area.

- What is the tone?
  Your piece is light but with underlying tones of bleakness. How much of that do you want the actor to capture?

- What does it tell you about character?
  If you have a scene where the character comes in very loud and brash, is it important to your vision that this comes across very strongly?

- What side of the character do we see?
  The character has a major gear change in the second act. Choose two scenes that allow you see both sides of the role.

If you have asked them to prepare a specific scene that is the turning point for the character, build up to this scene, rather than asking an actor to read/perform it **cold**.

Cold
Asking an actor to read with no preparation.

An example of working with an actor in an audition

On the following page you will find an excerpt from a scene from Shakespeare's 'Romeo & Juliet' to which we have added director's notes exploring the shape of the scene. This is followed by some ideas of how you could ask an actor to try different ways of playing it.

INT. BEDROOM IN VERONA - MORNING

                    JULIET
          Wilt thou be gone? It is not yet near day.
          It was the nightingale and not the lark
          that pierc-d the fearful hollow of thine ear.
          Nightly she sings on yond pomegranate tree.
          Believe me, love, it was the nightingale.

(JULIET IS DETERMINED TO PERSUADE ROMEO TO STAY)

                    ROMEO
          It was the lark, the herald of the morn,
          no nightingale. Look, love, what envious streaks
          do lace the severing clouds in yonder east.
          Night's candles are burnt out, and jocund day
          Stands tiptoe on the misty mountain tops.
          I must be gone and live, or stay and die.

(SEE ROMEO'S SENSE OF REAL DANGER ABOUT THE SITUATION)

                    JULIET
          It is some meteor that the sun exhales
          To be to thee this night a torchbearer
          And light thee on they way to Mantua.
          Therefore stay yet: thou need'st not to be gone.

(JULIET ENTICES ROMEO BACK INTO THE BEDROOM)

                    ROMEO
          Let me be ta'en, let me be put to death,
          I am content, so thou wilt have it so.
          I have more care to stay than will to go.
          Come death, and welcome. Juliet wills it so.
          How is't, my soul? Let's talk. It is not day.

(ROMEO CAN'T RESIST HER, HE TEASES HER AND SHOWS HIS PASSION)

                    JULIET
          It is, it is. Hie hence, begone, away.
          It is the lark that sings so out of tune,
          Straining harsh discords and unpleasing sharps.
          Some say the lark makes sweet division.
          This doth not so, for she divideth us.
          O now be gone, more light and light it grows.

(JULIET BECOMES DESPERATELY FEARFUL)

                    ROMEO
          More light and light: more dark and dark our woes.

(ROMEO BECOMES DARKER AND MORE SERIOUS THAN WE HAVE SEEN HIM)

ROMEO EXITS.

☐   How to approach this scene when working with actors

For the part of JULIET –

Since there are so many ways that the actor could approach this scene, as director, you need to decide how you want to explore it with the actor to see if you can successfully communicate what you are aiming for, as well as enabling you to see their range as an actor. You might ask the actor reading Juliet to be:

demanding, seductive, frustrated, amused, teasing or bossy.

For the part of ROMEO –

Similarly, think about the different ways an actor reading for Romeo could approach this scene. You could ask him to be:

arrogant, pleading, joking, nervous, passionate, panicking.

Always know what you want to explore when working on a scene with actors. Be ready to ask for specificity in the scene, in order to see the individual actor's qualities.

An actor might hit every beat, capture the tone, and embody the character as you see it. Equally, an actor may surprise you and bring something to the role that challenges and changes your perception of the character. You need to remain flexible and open-minded.

How many times should you read the scene?

Always ask them to do it more than once, so that they feel that they have had an opportunity to show an alternative to their initial reading. They might have travelled some distance to meet you. So make it a worthwhile exercise.'

Marina Caldarone – director

Ask the actor to read each scene at least twice. The first reading allows the actor to relax into the scene and you have an opportunity to hear their take on it. Then you can give them notes and direction, and ask them to read it again to see what else they do and also, very importantly, how well they respond to your direction.

It may be that each read is illuminating and exciting, and more ideas and ways of doing the scene are tumbling over themselves to be tried out, so you will want to work the scene four or five times. This is great and exciting.

However, unless you have given yourself enough time to workshop the scenes in this way, then it is best to arrange another session for a later date, rather than running behind and throwing out the timings of the rest of the casting session.

How to ask for what you want?

> *The actor is in a vulnerable situation, and it's your job to break down the initial barriers, to make them feel that you are working together on something, rather than that you are judging them.*
>
> Damien Goodwin – director

You need to be brave enough to ask for what you want. Actors need and want notes to improve their work but only if they are given in a helpful and positive way.

Below are some ideas of how to work with the actor on a script. We are using a film example and a theatre example. Ultimately, how you work is subjective and different for every director but these might help to get the ball rolling.

■   AUDITION EXAMPLE 1

If an actor has given a really internal, quiet read of the key emotional scene, which you really liked but hadn't been thinking of it in that way, you could ask them to:

■   *show* you more of what the character is feeling

■   change the physicality – if they sat for the first reading, then ask them to stand; if they were standing still ask them to move around

■   try a key moment in a different way – i.e. instead of being inwardly upset and quiet on a certain line, get outwardly very angry.

> *What you want at the audition is for the actor to present you with their view. You want to know if they can take direction, so the director will ask them to do something differently, to see if they can alter their performance.*
>
> Jo Ward – producer

■   AUDITION EXAMPLE 2

An actor has given a convincing, but very intense, reading of a scene but you are worried that she hasn't got the lightness that you were thinking about for the part. So ask her to do it again, but this time ask her to play the whole scene as if:

■   she finds something very funny about the whole situation – speaking through laughter, smiles or giggles

■   she is doing the washing up/making a bed/waiting for a bus/on the bus

■   she is on the verge of hysteria.

In this way she will be focussing on something other than her interpretation and you will be able to see her range.

Film Reading

Big
The screen can magnify every expression, potentially making a performance appear unbelievable.

Sometimes a performance may look a little too **big** on screen. This can happen if an actor has been doing a lot of theatre work. Don't be afraid to ask the actor to read it again, and ask them to internalize the thoughts. Suggest they 'think it, don't do it'.

☐   Is this the appropriate actor for your project?

If you are worried that an actor you really like hasn't shown vital aspects of the character, despite your direction, be realistic. If you only have three days to shoot and little or no rehearsal time, in these circumstances, the actor may not be the right one for you. You will not have enough time on set, so you will need to decide whether to go with the actor's take on the character, or choose another actor.

Theatre Reading

You see an actor you like but their most recent job has been working on screen. Therefore, they are used to producing work that is very internal, whereas you need them to communicate to an audience of anything from 50 to 500 people.

Ask them to read again but this time, perhaps get them to stand on the other side of the room. For stage work they will need skills such as voice projection, physicality and presence to reach their audience.

You have a better chance of developing a performance for a live production, as you may have anything from a week to six weeks rehearsal. So here you could take the risk that, with rehearsal time, you will be able to work with the actor to get what you want.

HOW TO BRING THE MEETING TO A CLOSE

☐ Do:

■ ask them if they have any questions
■ thank them for coming
■ tell them when they will hear from you
■ show them to the door
■ wait until they leave the room before making notes.

☐ Do not:

■ forget to thank them for coming
■ ask them to tell the next person to come in
■ start talking about them before they leave the room
■ get out the next actor's CV before they leave the room
■ yawn.

Before you invite the next actor into the room, ensure all the team have had time to write notes. By the end of the day, you won't be able to remember the detail of each actor and your notes will be important to help you make the final decision.

A pencil sketch

Remember that in a casting session you will not be getting a fully formed character and polished performance from the actor. The performance can, should and will change. Unlike you, they have not been living, dreaming and breathing the project for a significant amount of time. So what they will be giving you can be compared to a pencil sketch, which will be based on their gut reaction to the script and the character they are reading.

If it is a play, remember you will have a whole rehearsal period to explore the possibilities. If it is for film, make time pre-filming to talk to the actor and once on set you should not expect them to get everything in the first take.

James Schamus talked to us about the director's job in a casting session.

Novice directors often believe that the 'right' actor will walk through the door. But there is no such thing as the 'right' actor. Sometimes, after a long day of casting, I'll ask: 'What did you think?' And I'll hear: 'So-and-so was good, but they didn't quite get it.' At which point I say: 'Well, you're a director – direct!' Some of the greatest performances in the films I've been involved with have been from actors whose first reads during the casting process were terribly off the mark. But the director watched and listened, gave some direction or notes, or just had a brief discussion, and the actor took flight the next time. Casting really is part of the directing process.

James Schamus – film producer/writer

A word about nerves... yours and theirs

Everybody suffers from their own version of nerves especially in an unfamiliar situation. Nerves are good – adrenalin will keep you on your toes and stop you being complacent, too laid-back or sloppy. Equally, remember actors will suffer from nerves too. Nerves and being nervous are a universal bond.

Nerves manifest themselves in different ways, and you need to learn how they affect you so you are prepared. Nerves can wipe a person of their personality causing them to come across as monosyllabic – or they do the opposite and the person becomes over chatty and hyper.

Bear the nerve factor in mind and give all actors the benefit of the doubt. If you have allowed enough time in your audition schedule, and follow the advice about taking time to chat and get to know the actor, then you will have given everyone a chance to get their nerves under control and to give their best.

Casting is, for me, realizing a story. It's telling stories.

Kate Rhodes James – casting director

CASE STUDY – THE HEAD OF CASTING

*Not many theatres can boast a whole department devoted to casting – but the complex programme that the Royal Shakespeare Company (RSC) runs requires a level of expertise and professionalism that is illustrated by **Hannah Miller**.*

HM: My job title is 'Head of Casting'. So I'm the casting director on certain projects as well as the managerial 'Head of Department' within the organization, which means I am involved in the artistic planning and programming for the company.

Very occasionally something will come with an actor attached, or we will try to get an actor attached before we commit to producing it. But the majority of the time we put together a season of work and I will be involved in a budgetary sense, by estimating how many actors I think we could do that set of plays with.

Obviously, you want the best possible people for your productions, you want to get high profile people but it's not about tipping into celebrity. You want people to come, to respond to the shows, and you want to broaden audiences. So you want to work with people who may attract people to the theatre who might not otherwise come.

My most important relationship is always with the individual directors, but I'm also working within a team.

At the moment (*June 2011*) I'm working on a project that goes into rehearsals in August and a symposium which will act as a preparation for a project that's happening in July – but is also preparation for rehearsals next April – and a West End transfer of *Matilda* which goes into rehearsal at the end of August. The most RSC-specific thing, is something that goes into rehearsal on 31 October 2012, has a very long rehearsal process and doesn't actually hit the stage until March 2013 but I'm starting on that now, about five months in advance.

Q: And is that a play?

HM: It's a cycle of three plays where all the cast has to be in all three – so that's a typical **cross-casting** core piece of programming for the Stratford season in the main space – the director and I have been considering our leads for about nine months.

Q: So, where you've got three shows to cross-cast, what does that mean?

HM: When the idea of the project came together, the first stage was to budget it. I was asked if it was possible to cast those three plays – including understudies – with a certain number of actors. We're probably going to have about eighteen actors and I need to work out which roles each of those eighteen actors will play in each of the three plays. I have to consider that actors would be interested in a nice variety of parts – not necessarily all leads, because that might be too heavy a workload as they all rehearse simultaneously. I want to ensure that the actors feel they are being stretched and used in a versatile way across the three productions – and also make sure that everyone gets a nice part at some point.

Q: How do you talk to each director?

HM: It's unusual on this one, because it's one director who's come up with the idea and he is leading the project. He is seeing it as cycle, not three separate productions, with a through-line between the three productions. We begin by talking about the ideas behind the production: is there something extraordinary which will really change the way I approach making up the list? The list will be made up of people who the director suggests: actors they've never worked with but they've always wanted to, actors they've worked with before and really loved working with, actors they've heard about, actors I've put into the mix and then, of course, actors that agents put into the mix and actors who suggest themselves.

With three directors, each of the three directors will suggest actors that they want the other directors to meet. So it's duplicating the conversation with three people and then seeing where the connections lie, because quite often there will be consistency across those conversations. Michael Boyd once described me as the 'ringmaster'.

I'm trying to serve each individual director and their production, and make sure I do the best job for them. I'm serving the whole ensemble and group of actors and making sure they've each got an interesting journey; and I'm serving the RSC and making sure that those productions represent the RSC, the community of actors, agents and colleagues across the whole organization and industry.

Q: And is there any collaboration between directors?

HM: Yes. Recently we've been able to do more auditions with a team of directors, auditioning all in the same room at the same time. From an actor's perspective that can be great because if you do well, you know that everyone has seen you.

Q: What do you ask the actors to do?

HM: The majority of the time, we ask them to read from the scripts rather than do pieces. And in a case when there are two, three plays being discussed, I will often just ask them to prepare for two because to prepare three is too much – two's quite hard, but at least it gives contrast. And then perhaps, if a director still wants to see them do something specific from their play, we'll do that as a recall, but we're trying to use everyone's time most effectively.

And as with any casting process you're trying to ensure that the actors do themselves justice and the directors can find out everything they need to find out. If that's a workshop audition, that's great... lovely. If a director doesn't feel comfortable auditioning with other directors in the room then we won't do that. Whether it's a 20 minute, 30 minute or hour long meeting – we will tailor the process to however the directors feel they can best do their job.

cross-casting
within a company, actors are cast to play different roles, in two or more plays, that are staged alternately and regularly over several weeks or months.

CHAPTER 9

THE SESSION PART 3

- ■ Note taking
- ■ Film
- ■ Theatre
- ■ Things to consider
- ■ Thinking time
- ■ Decisions
- ■ Casting, the actor and the law
- ☐ Case study – The independent film producer

■ THE SESSION PART 3

> *How does anyone judge an actor's potential? Well, instinct is certainly involved but I would look for three major qualities: the skill to convince an audience of a character's psychology, the ability to engage them on an emotional level and the possession of a potent physical presence.*
>
> Sue Whatmough – casting director/producer

This chapter takes you through the final part of the audition process – deciding who to cast.

You have met your actors and you have some serious contenders for the roles. The next stage is to have a feedback session with the other members of your team, to find out what they thought and why.

NOTE TAKING

During the session the creative team needs to have been very focussed on each individual actor: responding to their questions, talking to them, watching and hearing them read. In between seeing each actor, every member of the team needs time to make notes.

Below is an example of a feedback chart which everyone present at our imaginary *Romeo and Juliet* casting has completed. It provides an excellent springboard to discuss each person's view and to compare notes.

> *Somebody comes in and physically hits the nail on the head – but if they can't deliver the dialogue and they can't get into the character, then it's not going to help at all.*
>
> Jo Ward – producer

Example Post Audition Feedback

	ACTOR A	ACTOR B	ACTOR C	ACTOR D
Part seen for	Juliet	Romeo	Juliet	Romeo
Initial thoughts	Very pretty, quite warm.	Was a bit cool and didn't seem to want to be there.	Hair much shorter than in photo.	Nothing like picture. Very smiley and open though.
Reaction to reading	Good – not as confident as I expected.	Quite hesitant – which might suit the part but…?	Really good reading – not what I expected though.	Fine – not great.
Qualities of actor	Quite open, very chatty. I liked her.	Doesn't look like photo, but very open.	Quite serious but very focussed.	Warm, open, likeable – but no passion?
Second reading thoughts	The same really.	Brilliant second read.	Not that much different.	Same as the first time.
Change/developed on second reading?	Not much, but then I quite liked what she did the first time.	Really exciting – completely changed it and 'got' what I wanted.	I didn't really ask her to change it as really liked what she did so just wanted to see it again.	I gave quite strong direction to be more excited and earnest – he didn't get it. We tried a couple of times.
Could you see her/him as the character?	Yes.	Yes – but wouldn't go with Actor A as Juliet – he looks a bit older.	Yes – would have to see if she would go with Actor B as Romeo though.	Not really – nice bloke but too laid-back and not got enough presence. Also still thinking about how brilliant Actor B was!
Recall or offer?	Depending on our Romeo really. HOLD.	Recall to work with Juliet. RECALL.	RECALL.	NO.

Here is a blank chart for you to fill in – make sure all the team who were in the casting session contribute their thoughts on each of the actors seen.

Post Audition Feedback Form

	ACTOR'S NAME	ACTOR'S NAME	ACTOR'S NAME	ACTOR'S NAME	ACTOR'S NAME	ACTOR'S NAME	ACTOR'S NAME	ACTOR'S NAME
Part seen for								
Initial thoughts *Were they what you expected in look or feel?*								
Reaction to reading *Was it what you expected?* *Did it surprise you?* *Were you excited/interested?* *Did you like their choices?*								
Qualities of actor *Your impression – does he/she match with your vision of the role?*								
Second reading *Did they carry out direction/notes?* *What effect did it have on their reading/the character?* *Was it better/worse/the same?*								
Overall *Could you work with them creatively?* *Did you like their thoughts on the project/character?* *Would they work with the other actors you have in mind or have cast?*								
Could you see actor as the character?								
Recall or offer or 'no'?								

FILM

I always watch the disc because it's very different when you watch what's been filmed.

John Griffin – executive producer

If your casting session was for a film, the most important thing you need to do is to review the recording of the actors.

This should be watched with all those who were present at the session. It is very interesting to see how an actor comes across when recorded as opposed to the impact they made in the room. Sometimes the difference is quite marked, as the camera may pick up a nuance or emotion that was missing when you watched them live.

Conversely, an actor might have been utterly spellbinding in the room – full of charisma, charm and energy – but when you watch the recording, you realise that none of the chemistry in the room comes across. This doesn't mean that the actor *can't* do it, and if you really like them, you should meet the actor again to work with them further and see if you can record the performance you want.

There are bound to be actors who gave a good reading but didn't really make your heart sing. Don't discount them. They may become your saviour when, due to circumstances, your first choice actors become unavailable and suddenly the actor who you initially thought was a bit predictable becomes the one who keeps the whole project afloat – and does an excellent job for you.

It isn't only one person's subjective view of how a character should look or be. There's always room for interpretations so it's quite interesting when you get to talk together and look at the footage at the end of the day.

Jo Ward – producer

THEATRE

With any casting process you're just trying to ensure that actors do themselves justice and the directors can find out everything they need to find out.

Hannah Miller – head of casting, RSC

With theatre it is equally important to have a de-brief and thinking period, and you also need to consider the dynamic between the actors, as they may be going to work together for a longer period of time, through rehearsals and performances.

THINGS TO CONSIDER

Quite apart from whether the actor blew you away with their reading and looked totally right, as discussed in earlier chapters, there are always other considerations. Are you casting best friends – would the two actors you like be believable together? It may be that you initially decided to see the actors in pairs as it is key that they have the right chemistry, or it may be that you have met actress A who could go with either actor B or actor C – in which case, it would be most sensible to get actress A to read with both actors B and C to see which combination works best for you.

> *Supposing you are casting siblings… they don't have to look identical, but there have to be certain similarities: you have to believe they are from the same family.*
>
> Jo Ward – producer

There might be an actor who you think is great and could do the part but you found it difficult to talk to them and they didn't take on board any of your notes. You saw another actor who was far more open and receptive but not quite what you were thinking of for this character. Which do you choose? You will need to take into account how much time you will have to work with them. Does it matter if you don't 'click'? This will depend on you: if you feel that they are perfect for the role, perhaps a personal connection won't be so important. But be sure to think through the reality of working with someone with whom you don't feel a rapport.

THINKING TIME

Once you have gathered your team's feedback, and if you are not in a crisis situation, it is incredibly useful to have a period to think about those you have seen and the team's reactions. It is always best to sleep on it – literally – and see how you feel the next day, before making any decisions.

DECISIONS

> *Casting is being creative and casting people in different roles from those they would ordinarily do. You reap the rewards of being a little dangerous with your craft.*
>
> Paul De Freitas – casting director

recall
asking an actor to a further audition for the same role.

If you are finding it really hard to make a decision, then this is the time to organize a second round of auditions and to **recall** those that you would like to meet again.

To recall or not to recall?

Actors don't get paid for auditioning, so be respectful and responsible and don't expect them to be hanging on the end of a phone, waiting for your call to come for yet another round of auditions.

If you are vacillating, give yourself a deadline and stick to it. Or get someone else to give you a deadline and ask them to make you stick to it.

☐   Reasons to recall:

■   the necessity of establishing chemistry between two roles
■   a huge lead role with many facets that you need to explore further
■   two brilliant choices – you want to work further with both.

It is not always necessary to recall and sometimes neither appropriate nor useful.

☐   Reasons not to recall:

■   feeling a bit lukewarm on an actor and hoping to be persuaded
■   panic
■   the role isn't working – admit it.

> *I find half a dozen of the best actors I can get, all different shapes and sizes, and then if we haven't got it, we'll know we haven't got it because we've missed a beat in the script.*
> Kate Rhodes James – casting director

Very often you will have little or no time to recall, or you might arrange a recall session only to find that the actors you ask back have been offered another job and so you are down to no actors and a deadline looming. This is why it is essential to meet several choices for a part:, so that if your first choice falls through – and your second – you have already seen someone who could do a good job, rather than letting panic ensue (at which point you would take any human being between 30 and 50 who could walk and talk!)

Contacting actors/agents after the casting session

Whatever the situation, you must *always* keep the agent/actor in touch with what is going on. This is excellent professional practice and people appreciate it. The next time you are in contact with that agent or actor, they will remember that you treated them with courtesy and professionalism, and they will be far more disposed to help you.

☐   For all actors you have seen:

Email or ring them to let them know what is going on. Here is an example of what you might say:

> 'Hi XXXX, just wanted to thank you so much for coming to meet us. It was great to hear your ideas and look at the scenes – we are still matching and mixing our cast and are aiming to let everyone know either way in the next XXXX days/weeks.'

☐   For those you are recalling:

As time is of the essence, *ring* the actor/agent to invite them for a recall and you will get an instant reaction and hopefully be able to confirm the meeting there and then.

> 'Hi XXXX, We really enjoyed the work you did. Would you be free to come back for a recall to work with the director in more depth? We will be meeting on XXXX (date) at XXXX (time) and the venue is XXXX (address). You will be meeting XXXX (director/producer etc.)'

☐   Making an offer:

You have decided to whom you want to offer the roles. Don't hang around – get on with offering them. Everyone likes to be told they have got a job! Ring the agent or the actor (if they don't have an agent), be enthusiastic and pleased and they will be too.

> 'Hi XXXX - We'd love you to do it! We'll send through a letter/email of confirmation.'

Then follow up with a confirmation email or letter with all the relevant details and contact numbers that they will need.

Dear *(name of agent or actor)*

Thank you so much for coming into meet us/read for us. We are delighted to offer you the part of *(name of part)* and are really looking forward to working with you.

Just to reiterate the details: We will be filming/rehearsing from *(date)* to *(date)*. The filming/rehearsing/playing will take place at *(name of venue/ town/street as appropriate)*.

Please could you get in touch *(either email or ring)* as soon as possible to let us know if you would like to do the job.

Many thanks and looking forward to hearing from you,

(your name)

If you don't hear from them within two or three days – ring/email again.

☐   Telling actors they haven't got the job:

This is as important as telling actors that they have got the job.

Only after the actor you are making an offer to has actually accepted the role, should you then contact the other actors you met to tell them that they didn't get it. *Don't do this too soon.* Wait until you are certain that your cast is rock solid which, in our experience, you can only be sure of when you are rehearsing or filming.

'Hi XXXX, thank you so much for coming in to see us. We really enjoyed meeting you but, sadly, on this occasion it is not going to work out. We really appreciate the time you put in and hope very much to work with you in the future. With best wishes...'

CASTING, THE ACTOR AND THE LAW

Whether or not you are offering the actor a fee, once they have said 'yes', the terms need to be agreed. This should be a conversation followed by a written confirmation.

The written confirmation should include the following details:

- overall dates of rehearsal and performance or filming
- venue/location
- fee and/or other remuneration (including the pledge of a dvd if it is a film)
- contact details of the team
- any other requirements.

On the following page we give you a template of a basic casting advice note, which we strongly recommend you create and complete for each member of your cast. This is excellent professional practice.

(Title of project)

CASTING ADVICE NOTE

(Date)
(Number of casting advice note)

Name: *(name of actor)*

Part: *(name of role)*

Address:

Tel:

Email:

Agent: *(if actor has an agent)*

Tel:

Email:

Fee: *(or expenses only/travel/profit share)*

Dates:

Any other stipulations agreed:

Asking actors to volunteer

If you are not in a position to pay your actors the agreed union rates, nor even the legal national minimum wage, you need to be aware that you are asking them to volunteer. That is, you are asking actors to donate their time, for no remuneration.

You are asking trained, dedicated, often experienced professionals – who have a living to earn, families to support and careers to nurture – to give you their time and expertise so that your project, and career, can prosper.

Hopefully, the actor will also get a lot from it. But you need to be aware of what you are asking and to ensure that you read the following guidelines. Treat the agreement between you and the actor with due care, diligence and respect.

Contracts

A contract is not necessarily a written piece of paper. It doesn't even have to be a verbal agreement. It is a description of a relationship. So you need to be sure that it is clear if the relationship you are entering into with the actor is one in which they are **volunteering.**

See the Appendices for an example of a volunteering agreement.

Tax & national insurance

If your actors are receiving nothing more than out-of-pocket expenses, then this reimbursement has no tax implications. However, if they receive *any* payment whatsoever, then this will be taxable. Just because you call it expenses doesn't make it exempt. You should always ask for receipts, before reimbursing expenses, and/or ask actors to complete an expenses claim form for volunteers.

Release forms

If you are making any kind of recorded media, whether or not you are paying your actors, you should always ask them to sign a **release form.** This is not the same as a contract of employment. It is essentially a license, which allows you to use the material (i.e. the performance) donated by the actor, within agreed limits.

See Appendices for useful websites that give examples of release forms.

Insurance

Whatever you are making – theatre, film, street theatre, site specific installation – you must ensure that actors are adequately insured.

Even if you are not employing your actors, you will still need insurance, and this means checking that existing policies extend to volunteers.

Safety and security

If you are a company with five or more employees, you will have a written health and safety policy. Ensure that volunteers are included in that policy. If you do not have a written policy, when you complete your risk assessment for your production, ensure that the volunteers' roles are included and that they have access to it.

Legal

Anyone involved in casting and engaging actors should make it their business to become familiar with the various industry agreements relevant to their specialism, because you need to ensure that your working conditions come as close as they possibly can to **industry standards**.

See the Appendices for useful information on industry organization details.

Case Study – the independent film producer

Marc Samuelson *is one of that rare breed of truly successful independent producers: making British films that regularly receive wide distribution and critical acclaim along with box office success.*

MS: With *Wilde* (1997), I wanted to make an honest film about the reality of what happened. And above everything else is the question 'who's he going to be?' because that's massive. Clearly you've got to have the right director; clearly you've got to have a brilliant screenplay and the right casting director. That was Sarah Bird, who did a brilliant, brilliant job.

The financiers wanted some kind of a star name and they made a lot of suggestions: Could it be Alfred Molina? Could it be John Malkovich? And you're thinking, 'Okay, that's interesting… really? It could be John Malkovich… hmmm… that's a very strange interpretation. Okay, let's keep discussing it. Could it be Brendan Gleeson? Well, maybe that's a bit more like it but not really etc.'

Sarah Bird was great friends with Lorraine Hamilton who represented Stephen Fry – who had always been talked about for doing an Oscar Wilde project. But the context of the time was that he'd walked off a West End play – *Cell Mates* – so I didn't even know if he was insurable, and he had no value internationally and I didn't know if he could act – but apart from that, he was ideal!

But Sarah and Lorraine persisted, so Brian (*Brian Gilbert, director*) and I went and had a drink with him… and four hours later we came out of the Savoy and I said to Stephen, you're my worst nightmare because I don't know if I can raise the money on you but I can't think of anybody else doing this – which I've never done in a meeting before but it was so obvious. And he left and Brian and I said to each other we need to just find a way to make this film with Stephen, no matter what, because he's just amazing and he personifies Wilde and brings a massive amount to it and I had no question, having met the man, that he'd be unreliable or flake out or be a problem à la *Cell Mates* and so on. And so we solved all those problems.

The great thing that Sarah did was… she knew that part of the job was going to be to deliver an ensemble of great actors, yes, but, frankly, they had to be an amazingly good looking group of young men. When we discussed Bosie, conceptually, Brian Gilbert said, 'The thing is – when he turns to the camera in the first shot, it's like the sun came out because you have to understand why Oscar was willing to throw his whole life away for this young man – even the straight men in the audience have got to get that.' To which Sarah said, 'Jude Law'. Just like that.

And it's really interesting because that level of certainty is unbelievably helpful – it cuts through it. This guy, Jude Law, he'd done next to nothing – he'd done one small movie, but Sarah had seen him on stage – in *Les Parents Terrible* – and said he was amazing, he's unbelievably good looking but the most important thing is that he's a really good actor. (So began the big debate about Jude Law, is he actually a character actor in the body of a leading man?)

We met him at my house – Stephen and Brian were sitting in my living room and the door bell rang, I'd never met this guy before and seen one photo of him, I opened the front door and I just thought, 'You're in!' because he was just absolutely right and indeed, he aced it in every way.

CHAPTER 10

CASTING CHILDREN

- ■ Practicalities
- ■ When to start?
- ■ Reading/audition
- ■ The workshop approach
- ■ Recalls
- ■ The law
- ☐ Case study – dramality

CASTING CHILDREN

> *Never work with children or animals.*
>
> W.C. Fields

Despite W.C. Fields' words of wisdom, children regularly appear on stage and screen. And they feature in many an iconic moment. This chapter takes you through what you need to know, what it means and how to go about casting children.

There are serious ethical considerations when you are involving children in your production. You should be very clear, from the outset, if there is any strong language, violence, sexual content or sensitive subject matter in your script. There must be total transparency so that an informed decision can be made on the child's behalf.

In the US there is far more work for child actors – Scarlett Johansson and Justin Timberlake were veterans by the time they were 12 years old, having started their careers at the age of four. The UK doesn't have the same opportunities for children so there are fewer places to see them acting. There are the most wonderful and natural young actors out there, but you will have to do your homework in order to find them. You may have to 'cast your net' widely.

What are you looking for?

You are looking for the right child to be convincing as the character you are casting. You will probably need them to learn lines and you will definitely need them to take direction. So you need to devise a way to establish their ability to do all those things.

PRACTICALITIES

Age

Always remember: in casting children it is not how old the child is, it is how old they *look*, especially given the discrepancies of height and size that can occur across several different age groups.

> *I've done zero to sixteen and sixteen to a hundred! You don't cast by the age the child is, you cast by the age the child looks.*
>
> Paul De Freitas – casting director

If you cast a child under the age of 16 you will have to obtain a licence and you will be restricted in the hours you will be allowed to work with them.

So start by being certain that you absolutely *need* to cast someone under the age of 16. If the character is written as 14 or 15 – for either stage or screen – always aim to cast older than 16. This could save you and your team a whole lot of time, administration and paperwork.

If your script needs younger children, say two key roles for children 'aged six', you should still aim to cast children who are older but who look the right age and have the right feel. Not only will this help you with the hours that the child can work, but, just as importantly, they will have greater maturity and focus.

■ **Always cast older children who look younger.**

If the writer has written some incidental children that are non-essential to the action, cut them – if at all possible – and make your life a lot easier.

■ **Never cast extraneous children.**

Casting children will have a major impact on the scheduling of your film or live performances.

■ **Be prepared and organized for the paperwork and administration.**

When to start?

You will need to start the casting process much sooner than for adult actors. Allow yourself a minimum of three months before the start of filming or rehearsals.

Here is a timeline example:

Filming dates mid-April (exact dates to be confirmed)

Script lock/ character breakdowns	Research and discussion	Children's workshops/ auditions	Recall workshops/ decision	Licensing paperwork	Licence granted/ production begins
January	Jan/Feb	End February	Beginning of March – mid-March	Mid-March – mid-April	April

Here is a timeline for you to fill in for your production.

■ Timeline for casting children

Remember to start your research no less than three months before your scheduled start of production.

Script lock/ character breakdowns	Research and discussion	Children's workshops/ auditions	Recall workshops/ decision	Licensing paperwork	Licence granted/ production begins

How to start looking?

The little boy from 'Pig Heart Boy' knew everything. He learnt it all, he delivered it beautifully, he took the notes.

Diana Kyle – producer

■ Children's Agencies

Start by seeing if there are any children's agencies in your area that you could contact. You can find details of children's agencies in CONTACTS and Spotlight publish a directory of *Spotlight Children and Young Performers*.

Approach a child's agent in the same way you would an adult actor's agent.

■ Stage Schools

There are a few, well-established, stage schools where the children fulfil their academic education alongside their training. There are also schools that focus on dance from an early age and all these can offer talented children who are confident and able performers. You can find details of these schools in CONTACTS and online.

■ Clubs and drama groups

All over the UK, there are dedicated clubs and societies where you will find children and young people taking part in the various disciplines of dancing, singing and music. These will vary according to where you live.

Investigate:

- your local theatre
- after school clubs
- Saturday clubs
- guides and scouts
- weekend drama groups
- amateur dramatic societies.

See Appendices for
listings of stage
schools and
children's drama
organizations

WHAT IS THE NEXT STEP?

☐   Send out a breakdown.

Use the same format as you would when contacting adult agencies.

☐   Send an introductory email.

Send an email, introducing yourself and giving a brief description
of the project and what you are looking for and then follow it up
with a phone call.

Here is an example of what you could put in an email:

> Dear XXXX (name of group/agent)
>
> My name is XXXX and I am writing from XXXX. I am currently preparing
> for a short film/theatre project and am looking for two children to play
> brother and sister between the ages of 8 and 12. If you have anyone who
> would be appropriate and interested, please let me know when would
> be convenient for me to ring for a chat to arrange to come in and see
> your classes at work.
>
> The filming/rehearsing/performance dates are XXXX. We would love to
> come in during the next two weeks if at all possible. This is a profit
> share/paid/expenses only production and we are attaching the script
> and a breakdown.
>
> Thank you so much for reading this email and we look forward to hearing
> from you soon.

☐   Make a phone call.

Talking to someone about your production is always the best way to progress and even more so when casting children.

Initially you will be contacting the person who is responsible for the children. They will need to be comfortable and reassured that you are legitimate and that the project you are working on is genuine. Be prepared for this, and always be totally clear about what you are asking for and from where you are calling.

Speak to the workshop leaders because they will know the members of the group and whether there are any likely candidates. They will help you identify who is suitable and arrange for you to visit the group, or for the children to come to a workshop you have organized. Remember that these people are doing you a favour and you need to be respectful and grateful for their time.

Phone call example:

                    YOU
          Hello. I'm YOUR NAME and I'm
          calling from NAME OF
          UNIVERSITY/GROUP/COMPANY. I'm
          currently casting for my
          FILM/THEATRE project and we are
          looking for NUMBER of children to
          appear. I wondered if I could talk
          to somebody about it?

                    YOUTH GROUP/AGENT
          Hi, what are you looking for?

                    YOU
          Well, we've got two roles - a boy
          and a girl. They are brother and
          sister and quite close in age.
          They are written as between 8 and
          10, so we're looking for children
          up to 11 or 12. Do you have any
          drama groups that have that age
          range?

                    YOUTH GROUP/AGENT
          Yes, we do. What would they have
          to do and what are the dates?

```
                    YOU
      The overall filming dates are X
      (date) to X (date) and we would
      only need them for X days
      filming/rehearsal/performance
      overall. We just wanted to get
      started early so we can get the
      licensing done in plenty of time.

              YOUTH GROUP/AGENT
      What would you like to do?

                    YOU
      It'd be great to come in and see
      them in their groups and then
      possibly arrange for a workshop
      with the ones we think would fit
      the bill and be interested in being
      involved.  Would that be possible?

              YOUTH GROUP/AGENT
      Okay, let's see if we can help and
      when would be a good day for you to
      come in.
```

Casting children can be a very laborious task, so being prepared is essential.

Attending a workshop

It is advisable and very worthwhile to attend a workshop or class that is being run by a youth theatre or group, in order to get a sense of the age range/look/types of children and whether they might fit into your idea of the character you are casting.

You want people who are dedicated and will be professional and understand that you don't just do it once and then you go home. You want people who want to be doing it, but it's not always great to have Cosette from Les Miserables at every audition. We often go for kids who go to drama school or drama clubs after school.

Jo Ward – producer

Attending a workshop will give you the opportunity to observe how the children interact with each other, how they look and move - and whether they have a spark that is interesting. It is always easier to observe children when they are in an environment where they are relaxed and unselfconscious.

Once you have observed a workshop, you can then shortlist to invite specific children to individual audition or group workshop. Both of these approaches have their own merits, and you need to decide which way is the best for you and your production.

You need to find out the same things as when casting adults:

- Do they have the right qualities?
- Can they take direction?
- Would you believe them in the role?
- Can you work with them?

And because they are children, there is the extra dimension of discovering whether:

- you can communicate with them
- they can relax and be natural
- they can sustain focus and concentration
- they have any necessary skills (i.e. singing/dancing).

READING/AUDITION

The audition process always works best when children are relaxed and a full explanation of what is required of them is clear and concise, leading to their increased confidence.
Valerie Jackson – agent/teacher, Stage 84

This way of auditioning may be more appropriate if you are dealing with children who have some screen or stage experience already and are familiar with the format.

Just as with adult actors, you should send out a script to the child's agent or parent, so they can have a read. Also, be sure to tell them – as you would with an adult actor – what scenes you will be looking at in the audition.

In the audition, have them read a scene from the script and give them some direction so you can gauge how ably they respond, and whether you will be able to work with them creatively.

We send them the script beforehand. So they've had a chance to read through it and understand what it is they're saying.
Jo Ward - producer

As ever the objective is to make the casting as relaxed and enjoyable as possible so that everyone comes across at their best.

I want them to be professional actors. They are told what the character is and what the series or program is. It's lovely when you get people who come in who are really prepared.

Diana Kyle – producer

THE WORKSHOP APPROACH

We often workshop them, because one audition doesn't give you all the information you need from a child.

Jo Ward – producer

To run a workshop, you will need to be organized. Look at your script and decide what you need to find out about the children and what your objectives are. Do they need to be very imaginative or confident? Do they need to be able to listen attentively and sit quietly, or be bossy, or cheeky?

Think about what games you might play which will help you to see if those qualities come easily to the children you are working with. And make sure you have a chance to actually give some direction, to see how they respond.

If you want to film the workshop you will need to ask permission of the workshop leader or the child's agent. Just as with filming castings with adult actors, be transparent and clear about what you are doing.

Nina Gold used this approach when casting for a child bully in *Happy-Go-Lucky*:

I did a workshop at the school we were using with the classes that were the right age. Some kids were much more into it than others – essentially they were doing their own thing.

Nina Gold – casting director

An example of a workshop audition for children

A workshop should never last more than 45 minutes. This example is designed for a group of ten children: five boys and five girls, all ranging in age between eight and eleven.

The brief is to find two children – a boy of ten and a girl of eight who will:

- *look like they could be brother and sister, having some physical resemblance*
- *work well together*
- *look the right ages/have the right age gap between them.*

The workshop plan is based on games and exercises related to actions carried out by the characters in the script and aims to help the director find out more about the personalities of the children at the workshop.

Games

(These would depend on size of the room, but aim to get one big enough for them to run about.)

Tig or catch

Objectives: to relax and energize a group.

One of the children is 'it' and has to catch other children – tap them on the shoulder – then that person becomes 'it'.

Variations on this game include:

the tagged person joining the 'it' person and then both trying to 'tag' everyone else in the room.

Grandmother footsteps

Objective: an opportunity to observe them without them being self-conscious. It is best not to film so that the children just concentrate on the game itself.

One child is 'Grandmother' and turns to face the wall. All the other children try to creep up on her from the opposite wall and tap her on the back without her seeing them move; if she turns round, they have to freeze and if she sees them moving, they have to go back to the wall and start again.

Treasure hunt

Objective: to find out who looks/works well together by observing them doing a 'real' task and being natural with each other. You could film them at certain points, as they interact with each other.

This is a version of a treasure hunt with the children working in pairs. Give them a map and have a few clues along the way. Have a time limit on certain clues, so you can retain control of the exercise.

Storytelling

Objective: to find out how much detail they can put into the story and how believable they are when they are telling it. Film the children listening to the story, as well as the child telling the story, to see how well they are concentrating.

All the children tell a story and the rest (including you) have to guess whether it is true or not. The children have to think of a story/incident and decide whether they are going to tell the truth or not – and write 'yes' or 'no' on a piece of paper (in this way they can't change it during the telling of it!). They give you the pieces of paper with their names written on them. Once the children have listened to each other's stories and asked questions, you then get them to vote as to whether they think each story is true or not. Once this is done, check the pieces of paper and see how believable their storytelling was.

A scene from the script

If there is dialogue, the scene will have been given to the group before the workshop.

Put the children into pairs according to who you would like to see work together. Ask them to read the scene quietly in pairs, so that they are not 'performing', and you go round each of the pairs, listen and then give them some direction. After that ask them to 'act it out' and film them at this stage. Be sure to give them some direction and work with any ideas that they have had.

■   Remember:

■   Ensure you have a comfortable environment to work in.
■   Don't make the workshop or audition too long.
■   Hear the children read with other actors if necessary.
■   Make it fun and relaxed.

Whether running an individual audition or a workshop, always be very clear in what you are asking the children to do.

> *Children often come in very nervous and the first thing you want to do is make them feel comfortable. You have got to give them a chance to do their best.*
>
> Jo Ward – producer

RECALLS

> *The casting process works best when it is fair, well organized, good communication is maintained between all parties and the children and their parents are put at ease.*
>
> Valerie Jackson – agent/teacher, Stage 84

As with adult actors, only recall if you absolutely need to. Hopefully, your audition process will result in you finding more than one choice that would work for you.

When you are casting children, it is essential that you have the time *once you have offered* to license and get all the forms prepared, so ideally you should be offering the role/s at least a month before shooting or rehearsal dates.

Producer Jo Ward talks about the casting process of Beaker Returns:

> *When you cast children you have got to have 21 days to get their licences and we only had 3 weeks to cast. We saw 160 kids over two days. Then we saw 80 in London and 80 in Manchester the following day. And we still didn't find everybody. We had more sessions and then we had workshops. We whittled them down and then ran workshops. Because you have to get the right balance of how they looked, their accents, ages and we still didn't feel that we were representing the population well enough - so we had some more sessions.*
>
> Jo Ward – producer

- Once you have found your children, made an offer and had it accepted, you must move quickly to apply for the licence from the local authority where the child lives.

  ☐ If it doesn't work out

As with any actor who has taken the time and effort to meet you, you must let the children know if they have not got the role. This should be done via their parents, guardian, agent or group leader in the form of an email or phone call.

THE LAW

The use of child actors, under the age of 16, in performances is regulated by the Children (Performances) Regulations 1968 and the 1963 Act. A licence must be obtained for a child for any performance that is recorded to be used in a broadcast or a film for public exhibition. Taking part as a performer in any rehearsal or preparation before the recording of a performance also brings the child under the licensing requirements.

All children under the age of 16 have strict restrictions on call times or length of 'continuous performance' and the maximum number of hours they can work per day including travel time.

- By law you will also need a chaperone. A chaperone can look after up to 12 children.

And also remember that there are different rules on how many hours you can work a child, depending on age.

See the Appendices for regulations regarding the hours children are allowed to work.

At the time of writing, the government has unveiled plans to change licensing laws for children working in the entertainment industry. The Department of Education say the new proposals have been designed to streamline existing legislation.

- Always check online to ensure that you are following the most up-to-date legislation.

The Licence

You will have to apply to the Education Department where the child lives, which will not necessarily be the same area as where they go to school.

There is a standard form to fill in and in order to complete this you will need:

- a photocopy of the child's birth certificate (if the child has not been licensed before)
- a letter of agreement from their school if they will be missing school days
- a doctor's letter (you might be charged for this)
- the parents to complete Part 2 of the form
- two passport sized photos of the child
- the completed and signed form.

You will also need to provide:

- details of locations
- schedules.

You will need to arrange for:

- a chaperone

and possibly

- a tutor – always double check the licence requirements.

The regulations apply if a UK child is performing abroad, or if a non-UK child is performing in the UK. Finally, once you have collated all your documentation you will need to allow at least 21 days for the licence to be processed.

Remember, even if you are casting your own child, or a friend's child, you will still need to apply for and obtain a licence from the local authority.

> *I said this is a job, this is a profession. We will have fun but it's not just fun and games. I need you to turn up on time, know the lines, do your best.*
>
> Diana Kyle – producer, *Grange Hill*

CHECKLIST FOR CHILD LICENSE

Make sure you go to the appropriate licensing authority – that is, where the child *lives* not where they go to school

ITEM	CHECK
Details and signature of parent	
Medical questionnaire completed and signed by parent	
Photographs of child (2 x identical photographs)	
Medical Certificate/Doctor's letter	
Original Birth Certificate	
Headteacher's permission	

Case Study – dramality

Damien Goodwin was Series Drama Producer on The Only Way is Essex. This role was created purely for the dramality genre. He used his experience as a drama director to oversee the final cut of the episodes and make them feel less like a reality series and more like drama.

Q: Is there a casting process in dramality?

DG: Yes, there is. As a form it lives or dies on the casting of the people within it. When *The Only Way is Essex* was conceived, one of the producers had to find a sample that would represent the cast. She went to Essex and met lots and lots of people and essentially she went through that process with the mentality of a someone who's putting together a drama.

In the first series, the strong male lead character was kind of an archetype of a white boy who couldn't really hold a relationship down. He kind of played the field and was someone to be reckoned with as far as the other guys in Essex were concerned. He had an attitude, a physical presence.

One of the things I worried about with him was whether he would come across as a sympathetic enough character, although he is very good looking and charismatic. They wanted to soften him and they found out that he had a pretty good relationship with his nanny. So we were in the process of casting and they realized they would have to bring her in as a subsidiary character – to soften him and make him more likable because you know you can't dislike a man who's being nice to his nanny!

No matter how badly he treats the women in his life as long as he's nice to his nanny... So that was a kind of a bit of a coup as far as that show is concerned because it made that character work on screen very, very well. The producers were kind of building a drama out of the characters they were meeting and realizing that what works on television as far as story telling is certain archetypes.

You had your bad guy; you had your funny sidekick who was constantly berated by the bad guy for not being as cool as he was and could never get the girls; on the opposite side you had the blonde siren who had this sort on-off relationship with the good guy... and essentially all of this is coming from their real life.

Really, the rules for casting for dramality are similar to the rules for casting for drama: you want to create conflict and you want your characters to be recognizable by your audience.

I think what's interesting is how filmmakers are starting to mix the world of actors and 'real' people in their filmmaking. Gareth Edward's *Monsters* is a very interesting film from that point of view. There are two central characters, or actors, and Edwards stopped at various places throughout Mexico, using authentic people from the region. And actually, they sat remarkably well together – the authenticity of the Mexicans made the American actors appear more authentic as well, and they did things that weren't necessarily predictable but were very real within the situation.

The frustrating thing about dramality, from the director's point of view, is that you can't move the characters around because you'd have problems with continuity. So, watching dramality you realize how static it is and that there's no motivated moves. But I do think that there is something to be learned from the cross germination of those two worlds, and how they can work in unison together, and how one feeds off the other.

CHAPTER 11

THE BUSINESS OF CASTING

- Film
- Theatre
- Television
- Radio
- Commercials
- Corporate
- Voice

■ THE BUSINESS OF CASTING

> *You can write 'the army came over the hill' but you might not be able to afford the army or the hill. So work out what your story is and how you can afford to tell it and then find the right people to interpret it for you – your cast. And live your vision.*
>
> Jo Ward – producer

There are as many different situations where casting occurs as there are actors to be cast. Think of anything where an actor is seen or heard (for example, telephone answer machines, station and train announcements and computer voices) and there will have been a casting decision made. This chapter gives a brief description of the process in all the different areas where casting occurs.

> *Someone just caught your eye. Make a note of who they are and have a think about 'why did they catch my eye?' What was it they did, try and analyse it a little bit and think what is attractive about them? Not necessarily in looks, but what was that something that caught your attention?*
>
> Beryl Vertue – producer, Hartswood Films

FILM

The proliferation of affordable equipment means that filmmaking is an industry that encompasses as many scales of production as there are filmmakers. In this section we will be looking at how casting works with different levels of budget.

Student films/lo–to–no budget films

Use what you have learned from this book and add imagination and ingenuity to find your perfect cast to make your film truly memorable.

> *If you are confident enough to approach an actor of calibre and say 'If you want to do this, it's yours. It's happening in two weeks' time' you'll have someone go 'Great script – not doing anything, okay, yeah, I'll give it a punt'. Whereas if you send someone a script saying 'It's happening in six months' time' then there's no way you'd get anyone.*
>
> Tim Welton – director/producer

A member of the production team should take on the job of casting director and be responsible for ensuring breakdowns are circulated, potential cast approached and followed up.

You may want to attract a high profile actor. Be brave. You will never know if your dream actor is available and interested if you don't ask. You will have to convince their agent to read the script first. Make sure you are prepared.

Independent/non-studio films

The vast majority of what you would understand as British independent films are put together by independent producers and they are starting with nothing, so they have to create the project from nothing and they have to raise all the money for it.

Marc Samuelson – producer

Very often the finance only kicks in after the cast, script and creative team are in place and, unless the director or producer/s have sufficient **marquee value**, it will normally be the actors who will attract that finance.

marquee value
A name that when advertised on billboards will have the power to attract an audience.

Independent productions are instigated by a producer – sometimes from a script brought to them by a writer or director – and they may have been working on it for many years. The producer puts in place all the key creative personnel.

The casting director often becomes attached to a project long before it is green lit, in order to deliver the cast that will get the film financed. Therefore the casting process can take as long as the development period – and that can take years!

Casting directors are like every other key creative member of the filmmaking team. Just like cinematographers, there are many wonderfully talented people out there – each has a personality, a signature, an approach.

James Schamus – screenwriter/producer

THEATRE

I have seen couple of things where I thought the lead casting just blew it. Luckily it doesn't happen very often. Casting is crucial. If you get the right cast, it can be just stunning.

Diana Kyle – producer

All you need to create a piece of theatre is a performer, the space and an audience. Good casting is vital. Every director and producer is looking for the right combination of skill, experience and talent to support and fulfil their ideas.

Student/fringe productions

It's all down to taste in the end.

David Grindrod – casting director

In this kind of theatre, the motivator and instigator is usually the director rather than the producer. They will have the vision and be the central figure in developing an idea. If there is a producer attached, they will oversee the budget and be involved in scheduling, marketing and, in some cases, work with the director on the casting.

The casting is generally done by the director, who may have certain actors in mind from the outset. Or the director may audition within a small geographical radius. It is unlikely that they would look further afield than a train or bus journey, due to requiring the actors to rehearse and perform locally over an extended period of time.

Subsidized theatre

This includes all theatre that receives public funding.

It's fantastic... because you've got lots of opportunities to make great work... it isn't just a theatre, it's a cultural centre for the area, so you can help a lot of things happen as well as your own productions – you can enable other people to realise their creative ambitions and that's the most exciting thing about it.

Joe Sumsion – artistic director

Regional theatre

In rep I played parts like Patrick in The Hostage, a man in his 60s – I was playing character roles that at the age of 25 you're not expecting to play, so I didn't get type cast by what I was being asked to do.

Vincent Franklin – actor

Repertory
A permanent company that produces regular work.

Regional theatre is exactly that – theatre that happens in the regions. Few regional theatres work on the traditional **repertory** system, where actors are resident for a season of different plays.

Contemporary regional repertory theatres tend to co-produce with other regional theatres in order to share costs and allow their audiences to benefit from high production values.

In regional theatre the producer is known as the Executive Director or Chief Executive. This is generally more of an administrative and financial role and less of a creative one. Where a regional theatre has an Artistic Director, they will be responsible for the artistic vision. In some theatres the Artistic Director is also the Chief Executive and responsible for creative, administrative and financial decisions. In the larger regional theatres, the Artistic Director will oversee the employment of freelance directors and designers who will work on one-off productions during a season.

> *It's changed because those theatres have gone, pretty much. There was kind of a sense of a company, but they went from doing nine shows a year to doing seven and instead of a cast of eight, there was a cast of six and a two hander in the middle, so there wasn't the opportunity to put a company together.*
>
> Vincent Franklin – actor

Casting usually happens production by production, because in buildings with more than one auditorium it would be impossible to **through-cast** as production times will vary and therefore so will the availability of the actor. Casting will also depend on the requirements of the show – a musical, for example, demands a different skill set than a community theatre tour or an open air Shakespeare.

Through-cast
An actor cast in a variety of roles in a season of plays.

A casting director can be employed on a particular production or to cast a season of shows. Some regional theatres have a resident casting director.

Where co-productions between theatres occur, a freelance casting director could be brought in specifically for the production.

Other regional theatres source actors through advertising on their website, by using Spotlight, or through one of the industry websites such as PCR or Casting Call Pro. The director of the production will normally handle the casting and will also have a pool of local actors to call upon.

Touring

Examples of touring companies are Kneehigh and Complicité, who work out of a permanent base, where their offices and rehearsal spaces are situated, and then tour nationally or internationally.

Casting is slightly different here, as they have a core company of actors who have a shared method and approach towards their work, which they have developed over a long period of time. There will be a pool of actors to choose from, as well as those actors writing speculative letters to the company, asking to be considered.

Royal Shakespeare Company/National Theatre

At both the RSC and the National there are permanent casting departments consisting of between three and five staff on long-term contracts. They deal with all the administration, organization and creativity involved in the complicated casting process.

At the National Theatre there are three fixed auditoria and each has a full season of plays all of which are cast by the casting department.

At the RSC the need to cast a repertoire of plays, which are performed over a long period of time, means that the casting department has to put together a company of actors who have the right experience, skills and temperament to work together for anything up to 24 months, in a variety of different venues – Stratford, London and on tour.

> *Working in-house you are within a department, so there is a team of four – another casting director, an assistant casting director and a casting administrator. As a department we have three different functions, we cast the plays, the readings, the events, and we also do all the contractual paperwork – everything.*
>
> Hannah Miller – head of casting, RSC

Each play in the season has its own director and each director will be looking for their perfect cast. They have to collaborate and compromise where necessary.

> *You want to see that an actor has been working with really good directors and in really big spaces – space is more of an issue. If somebody has only worked in Bush size spaces, that's more of an issue because we need to sort of test them in a way – whereas with an actor who has worked in various big spaces, then you're looking for different things.*
>
> Hannah Miller – head of casting, RSC

Commercial theatre

The one thing over everything else in commercial theatre, is that the audience are the gods, they really are. There is a contract with the audience and we listen to them afterwards.

Tim Welton – director/producer

Commercial theatre is theatre that is not publicly funded. In London some of the big producers, such as ATG (Ambassadors Theatre Group) and Nimax, own theatre buildings, whilst others, such as Fiery Angel, David Pugh and Bill Kenwright, produce the shows and book them into theatres.

Producers come up with an idea, find the money and decide on the creative team, maintaining overall control. Financing comes from private investors who hope and want to make a profit on their investment. This means attracting maximum box office revenue, so producers will be looking for actors that audiences will recognize. Sometimes a **number 1 tour** will look for a recognition factor by casting a non–acting celebrity (anyone from a TV chef to a football star) and then casting experienced actors to support them.

Number 1 tour
A touring theatre production which goes to major theatres in large cities nationally.

Commercial theatre is a strange hybrid between cutting edge and very, very old fashioned ideas.

Tim Welton – director/producer

The director and casting director are usually employed by the producer, although the casting of the leads is often decided prior to the director coming on board. As with independent filmmaking, a star name can ensure that the production goes ahead, so securing that name is the first priority of the producer and casting director.

In commercial theatre casting directors have to cast all named parts and understudies, and actors often understudy more than one role.

Musicals

Musical theatre is a thriving business and significant industry employer. There are normally several large scale productions touring at any one time, as well as the massive on-going musicals in London.

We asked David Grindrod about the process of casting musicals:

Q: What is the average number of cast on your big shows?

DG: Around 30. It's quite a big jigsaw puzzle to put together.

Q: And where do you start with that jigsaw puzzle?

DG: You start from the script development workshops and get an idea from that. We're currently doing a musical based on the Spice Girls – so we'll go to the drama schools and colleges and see their third year students – we'll need that youthful quality. Or there's the speciality thing – we've been doing *How to Train Your Dragon* and that was all to do with aerial skills – are they good on wires, on silks? So we had to go for circus performers.

Q: What's the prep time on that?

DG: It depends. How long's a piece of string! But when you're casting a musical from scratch, it's about four to six weeks, hopefully, from beginning to end.

Q: But that could be a project that's been two and a half years in development? So you have had time to think?

DG: Correct.

All performers in musicals have to be able to produce a consistently high standard of acting, singing and dancing and maintain it for 8 shows a week, 52 weeks a year. There are courses specifically designed to train actors for this type of physically and musically demanding work.

Producers are responsible for putting together the creative team and the finance – often a consortium as musicals are an expensive business to fund.

The casting director is employed to find the opening cast and will be responsible for re-casting long-running shows, at least every 12 months. Certain casting directors specialize in casting musicals and have an encyclopaedic knowledge of actors for that genre.

TELEVISION CASTING

Casting is the fun bit. You've slaved away. Draft upon draft upon draft. The first time that somebody says those words and makes them real, it suddenly takes on a whole different dimension. I like actors and everybody comes with different interpretations and it's really exciting. It's the best bit!

Jo Ward – producer

Casting for television can involve decisions being made by a raft of directors, producers, executive producers, series producers, drama controllers and network chiefs, all with a level of responsibility for what is broadcast to the viewers.

The casting director has to understand the demands of the broadcasters and the commissioning channel, as well as satisfy the expectations of the production company. For example, the casting required for a major BBC1 drama series transmitting on a Saturday night, will differ from an edgy Channel 4 show or a children's series for CBBC.

The decision making process can be long, sometimes with actors being recalled on several occasions in order for everyone to be satisfied that they are getting exactly the right actor for their show.

Single drama and series television

At the centre of it is the producer. They are the project manager. They may seem to do little, but they are responsible for everything. It's not unlike the project manager on a building site who doesn't actually build anything but is responsible for every brick being in the right place and that it comes in on budget. That's what a producer does.

John Griffin – executive producer

Single dramas and series are usually produced by a team specifically contracted for those productions by an independent production company who have been commissioned by a broadcaster, for example by Channel 4 or the BBC.

The management and structure for casting decisions is as follows:

■ An executive producer/s representing the companies investing in the production.

- An executive producer/s from the production company who are physically producing.

- An executive producer/s representing the different production company (or companies) involved in the finance.

- An executive producer/s representing the broadcaster.

- A producer putting together the creative team who could have been involved since inception or might have been brought on board by the production company at a later stage. On a series there is usually one producer who oversees the whole production.

- A director – in series dramas there is usually one lead director responsible for deciding the regular cast. If there are more directors on board for subsequent episodes, they will also be involved in the episodic casting.

- A casting director who was recommended by the producer or by the production company. As the casting director and director are **for hire** they won't necessarily have an established working relationship.

For hire
Any professional who is employed to work on a project, as opposed to instigating and developing it.

Serial television or continuing drama

I'm responsible for delivering the programme to the Executives and the Channel Commissioner. Everybody reports to me. I liaise with them all and the casting director is as important as everybody else on the team.

Diana Kyle – producer

Serial television is broadcast on a weekly, bi-weekly or daily series basis. The stories revolve around a group of characters with the focus moving from character to character. *Holby, Casualty, Coronation Street* and *Emmerdale* fall into this category.

- An executive producer/s overseeing the whole process and having the final say on casting of **regular characters.**

Regular characters
Characters that recur in a series or serial.

- A series producer who is responsible for the on-going content and major casting choices.

■ A producer working on a **block of episodes** who is closely involved in the day-to-day business of the production, including casting.

Block (of episodes)
More than one episode, but less than an entire series.

■ A casting director working on the whole series, possibly with an associate or assistant, responsible for new regular characters that are coming into the show as well as any incidental or short-running storylines.

My main contact in the complex production structure is an executive producer/s who manages the show for the broadcaster or independent company. I try to develop a trusting relationship with them so that I can manage and invest the creative talents within the programme, to deliver what is wanted as I think best. Generally the director is the creative catalyst on the floor but I am technically senior as there are production issues that I need to be across too.

Tim Bradley – producer

Depending on the channel, the casting director will either do the deals on the actors, or they will be done by a centralized contracts department, who are responsible for all in-house productions.

Drama Documentary

This is when a script is written using real-life characters and actors are cast to play them.

When I was casting for the D-Day film, I was working from the real-life descriptions of the veterans involved. I was matching their qualities and energies to the actors I found. The interesting thing was that many of the actors who ended up portraying real-life veterans looked uncannily like them.

Suzy Catliff – casting director

Documentary

Documentaries tell a story just as much as any fiction film or TV drama. The story needs to be told by strong, charismatic and engaging characters and the job of the documentary producer or director is to find the ideal person who can be natural in front of the camera.

We talked to documentary filmmaker Tim Schwab:

Casting a documentary – choosing your subjects – is one of the key creative decisions made in preparing a character driven documentary. The main subject or subjects set the whole tone of the film, usually driving both the content and the presentation of the content, meaning that the whole creative approach flows out of the people you are choosing to focus on. They become the face and the voice of the film, and the major aesthetic and editorial decisions will flow from the filmmakers' relationship with those subjects and the force of their stories and personalities.

If you are doing a subject or character centred documentary, you do in a sense 'cast' it, as you are making selections about using this person rather than that person. Sometimes this is done for you, as you pick a certain character because there is something interesting or unique about them that you are going to build a story around.

Or, if you have an idea or theme, you need to populate it with people who will advance the structure and content of the film. You may talk to a large number of people in doing background research, and then select a few of them to be in the film, based on how articulate they are; how representative they are of the overall group being examined; how they look; how their stories intersect with the theme of the project; their degree of ease on camera; the degree of access you have to them; the visual opportunities offered by where they live or work or what they do.

Dramality

Dramality is a hybrid form of storytelling, mixing documentary and reality television, and is played out in real time. The characters play themselves or a version of themselves which has been edited by a professional team of programme makers.

The casting of this type of show, and the chemistry of the characters, is always going to be crucial to its success, just as with any casting for a major Hollywood blockbuster.

- A producer pitches the idea to a production company who will then pitch it to a broadcaster once the producer, and their team, have done the research and found the subjects (the cast).
- As this type of work does not call for actors, the casting is not done by a drama casting director but by the producer and researchers.

RADIO CASTING

I think there's a pressure on individual producers to use some element of recognizability in their casting because the press doesn't pick up on radio drama unless they recognize the actor's name. For example, I recently did a production that had Kenneth Branagh in it. Kenneth hardly ever does radio, and he's a film star, and so immediately the noticeability of that production rose by 10 per cent. However, there is no evidence that this type of casting increases listening figures. In fact many keen radio listeners say, 'I prefer not to know who the actors are because it interferes with my mental pictures and I enjoy listening to radio because of the pictures it paints in my mind'.

Alison Hindell – Head of BBC Audio Drama

Most radio drama is heard on the BBC. As with television there are long-running series, such as *The Archers*, with a regular cast of characters – some of the actors have played their character for over 30 years.

The BBC has their own drama department and studios, and are significant producers of drama radio output. Every day there is at least one new play transmitted as well as series and single plays. Freelance, independent directors and producers can take their ideas to production companies, who will then adopt the project and pitch it to the most suitable editor or commissioner.

- The producer is responsible for overseeing the creative team and scheduling issues.

There are radio drama producers based all around the country. By and large those people will be recording in their local studio and recruiting from local actors. In London it's slightly different because there's a bigger pool of actors to call on and also the London department runs the Radio Drama Company who, although they are a resource for everyone around the country, are primarily used on a day-to-day, play-as-cast basis in London.

Alison Hindell – Head of BBC Audio Drama

The director is responsible for casting. Because the turnaround is so quick, casting directors are not generally employed for radio and, as the actor is only needed for a few hours work, there is a wider pool of actors to call on.

The contracts are very short, a half day, a day and a half, three days at the most. We might meet for cup of tea or have a chat over the phone, so that I can hear that the voice isn't going to be anything like another actor's in the piece. And, of course, their voice clip on Spotlight is the perfect first port of call, in terms of their casting eligibility for the role.

Marina Caldarone – director

COMMERCIALS CASTING

Casting for commercials can involve casting models, children and actors. The primary concern of the client is to find the right image to sell the product, which will be aimed at a specific demographic.

There's the client, who wants to launch his new brand. He goes to an advertising agency and they write the script, and then the advertising agency go to a production company, And then they send the script to me, the casting director, and the producer pencils me in. Sometimes they can ring you on the Monday and want the casting on the Tuesday – as short notice as that. Years ago, before the advent of computers, they'd have pencilled you in a couple of weeks in advance. The money has always been quite good on commercials because you're being paid for the short notice and the stress.

Paul De Freitas – casting director

Commercials can be very expensive to make, with budgets rivalling that of feature films. Casting directors are employed by the production company/producer. Casting for commercials is a high octane, quick turnover of potential faces or bodies and takes place very quickly.

CORPORATE CASTING

Corporates are informational films or live performances, specifically written and aimed at a target audience. Corporates use actors to act in a film or take part in interactive role play with employees.

VOICE CASTING

With the voices you know that you've got actors who are great at doing multi-characters, so they can do a variety of accents and are able to play old and young, quirky and funny. There's a quite a number of actors who specialize in playing ten-year-old boys or girls.

Damien Goodwin – director

Everything you *hear* on television, radio or films – a voice-over on an MFI advert, a trailer for a new drama series or the latest video game – has been cast. There are voice-over agencies who specifically deal with actors' voices. In many ways, it is a far simpler process than most other forms of casting, as the producer or director can easily go online and listen to a selection of voices and make a decision.

Video games and animation:

> *The last game I directed there were 512 different characters and there were 27 actors filling all those roles.*
>
> Damien Goodwin – director

Actors are contracted in the development stages, and are sometimes on board for years, working in motion capture studios with directors, creating the characters for the animators to work from. Once the games are completed, a director is brought on board to direct the voicing of the game.

■ QUOTES AND CASE STUDIES – THE INTERVIEWEES

The advice we bring you is from every area of the industry that has any connection to casting. Take time to read about these practitioners and get to know them a little so that you understand the context of their comments.

CASTING DIRECTORS

Paul De Freitas – Freelance
I was a child actor from the age of ten. I was one of Sylvia Young's – a very well-known child agent and drama school now. I was one of her first pupils, where I developed a bit of a personality and lost my cockney accent. I did bits of acting as a child: Peter Pan *at the Palladium; the* Fun Food Factory *– a kids TV series;* Bugsy Malone *with Alan Parker and then, when I was about 14 or 15, I met a casting director, who said 'Why don't you come in your six week holidays and help me out a little bit?', which I did, and when I was 16, he offered me a full time job. I stayed with him as an assistant and cast lots of commercials. The plan was to go back to acting but I never did, so, at 23, I left and set up on my own.*

Nina Gold – TV and film
Nina's recent film credits include: *Les Miserables, The Kings Speech, Prometheus, The Iron Lady* and *The Chronicles of Narnia.* Recent TV credits include: *Game of Thrones, Rome* and *Coup.* She has had a long working collaboration with Mike Leigh, including the films *Vera Drake, Happy-Go-Lucky* and *Topsy Turvy.*

David Grindrod – (Mamma Mia!, Shrek, Ghost, Jesus Christ Superstar, Viva Forever)
I went to LAMDA, trained as a stage manager and went into two weekly rep for 40 weeks to get my Equity card so I could come to into London. I moved to the Royal Court and then joined the RSC, starting off as Assistant Stage Manager and ending up as Company Manager. I went to Chichester for two years, left Chichester with La Cage Aux Folles, *then company managed* Starlight Express *in Japan and Australia, then three more years for*

Duncan Weldon Productions. Andrew Treagus asked 'Would you organize a school choir competition within the bounds of the M25 area and can we leave that to you?' It took me about six months to set up a school choir thing around the M25 area, we opened the show Joseph and his Amazing Technicolor Dreamcoat *with Jason Donovan. It was a huge success and I got asked to join the company – the Really Useful Group itself. We did* Sunset Boulevard *which I general managed then, for the second company, they asked me to cast it and that's kind of how I got started on the musicals.*

Doreen Jones – Freelance (Brideshead Revisited, Prime Suspect, Wallander)

Doreen started at Granada and stayed to become Head of Casting and now works as a freelance casting director. In 2006 Doreen won an EMMY TV award for her casting of the TV series *Elizabeth*. She works extensively in television on both series and single dramas. She was one of the founders of the Casting Directors Guild.

Hannah Miller – Head of Casting, RSC

I did a drama degree at Hull University and did lots of Edinburgh Festivals, lots of National Student Drama Festivals – I did 33 productions over three years, I remember working that out! But I did everything – I did very little acting but I directed, I produced, I stage managed, I did costume design, lighting design, literally everything – at some point or another.

Nadine Rennie – Soho Theatre

I'm a theatre director and that's how I came to it. I got a job at Soho Theatre on a tour of Amanda Whittington's Be My Baby. *I was Abigail Morris's assistant on that and at that same time her then PA here in the building at Soho Theatre was leaving, and she said to me 'Would you come in and cover for a few weeks while we look for a replacement?' She knew when I wasn't directing I would temp as a PA around town. So I did that and it kind of.... I'm still here really.*

Kate Rhodes James– (Bleak House, Sherlock, Titanic miniseries)

I went to drama school, but it became apparent that I wasn't destined to be an actress. I adored the industry and wanted to take an active role. I met the casting director on Young Indiana Chronicles *and was offered the position of her assistant – and I never looked back. I absolutely adored it.*

Sue Whatmough – Casting director/producer
Sue started working on the stage door at the Old Vic Theatre and then the Mermaid Theatre, where she later became casting director. From there she moved into film and television and, over 25 years, cast a wide range of drama and comedy before becoming a producer. Most notably, she packaged and co-produced the drama series *Blott on the Landscape*. In the first part of her autobiography *No Copy of the Script*, she details the casting process based on her experiences.

ACTORS

Vincent Franklin – (The Office, Twenty Twelve, Confetti, In The Thick of It, Topsy Turvy)
I graduated in 1990 from Bristol Old Vic Theatre School. I began by doing lots and lots of theatre and then wanted to have kids and not be disappearing off working six days a week in the middle of nowhere. So then I concentrated on television, because I'd got wrapped up in spending a long time in the same theatre companies often going back and doing different parts.

Angela Lonsdale – (Coronation Street, Casualty, Doctors, The Bill)
Youth theatre, in Cumbria, is probably where I first started, at the Brewery Arts centre. I went to drama school – Royal Scottish Academy in Glasgow – then when I left there, my first job was Theatre in Education, then I went to Northern Stage for three years. Then I got my first telly break, Finney *with David Hayman, and then sort of went down the telly road after that and have done various bits: 'Corrie',* The Bill, Doctors, Kavanagh QC. *And bits of theatre in between.*

Sasha Morphitis – (Lucky Stiff, Live for the Moment, Silent Witness)
Sasha received a BA in Classics at Reading University then trained at Mountview Academy of Theatre Arts, BA (Hons) in Musical Theatre. Her theatre work includes Alice Fitzwaren in *Dick Whittington*, *Past Tense* (new writing), *Lucky Stiff* (Wimbledon Studio) and *The Wiz* (Gatehouse). Her film work includes: *Live for the Moment* and the BAFTA winning short film *Do Not Erase*. Her TV work includes: *Silent Witness*. Sasha is currently working as a primary school teacher and mother.

Jason O'Mara – (Monarch of the Glen, Terra Nova, The Agency, RSC)
Jason completed a four-year BA in Drama and Theatre at the Samuel Beckett Centre for Performing Arts, Trinity College in Dublin. He worked for the RSC and in regional repertory theatre and various TV series, including *Monarch of the Glen* and *Band of Brothers*. Jason starred in the US version of *Life on Mars* and as Jim Shannon in Spielberg's *Terra Nova*. Jason says 'I got an audition for a period drama for the BBC called *Berkeley Square*. That was my first TV break and I really got into a nice balance of doing a theatre job here and going to do a TV job there. I think probably the ideal situation for any actor, or at the least the kind of actor I am, is to have a balance of doing TV and theatre.'

Ruby Snape – (Holby City, The Grimleys, Bodies)
Ruby trained at Guildford School of Acting, and has worked in a variety of theatre, TV and commercial roles including Miss Thing in *The Grimleys*, *Holby City* and *Bodies* as well as having many theatre credits. Ruby also runs her own freelance events company.

AGENTS

Jeremy Brook – Jeremy Brook Ltd
I started in 1988 when I went to the Central School of Speech and Drama and left there a little bit early to do a television job and worked fairly steadily for about six or seven years. I thought it would be very difficult to use my skills as an actor, and you sometimes think you haven't got a lot to offer outside of the acting thing, but actually you have – a big basic sort of general knowledge of literature. You're able to talk to actors about auditions, preparation, about acting itself, performance, you can tell them something of your experiences, which some of them very often haven't even touched upon. So I found there was a lot I had to offer to the actors on the agency list, and then I got an offer from my own agent to go and work for her as an assistant.

Victoria Futcher – Agent, Lou Coulson Associates
I studied drama and theatre at university – Royal Holloway. The only thing I knew was that I didn't want to act. I moved to London and did any job I could. Then I heard the Lou was looking for an administration assistant, so I got that and then a year later an agent left and I got moved up to be an agent – and that was seven years ago.

Jean Diamond – Diamond Management Ltd
Jean Diamond began her long career in the entertainment world as
a junior in the literary department of the largest international
agency of the day, MCA. Within a few months she took over the
running of the repertory rights to all the catalogue of their client
plays – including *Dial M for Murder*, which was released at this
time. Whilst at MCA she was offered the chance to be the assistant
casting director for MGM Studios, and was later promoted to
casting director. She worked with many great directors on many
wonderful films including *Ben Hur, Dunkirk* and *Bhowani
Junction*. After three years she was invited to for a new agency –
London Management – with two partners, which became one of
the top three agencies in the country. In 2003, she decided to
return to the boutique style of agency management, and founded
Diamond Management with business partner Lesley Duff. Her
illustrious client list has included Denholm Elliot, Ian Richardson,
Max Von Sydow and Charlotte Rampling.

Valerie Jackson – Agent/teacher, Stage 84
Valerie founded Stage 84 in 1984 and the school is one of the most
successful and well known for performing arts in the north of
England. Her students regularly appear in television series and
dramas and have performed in all of the major musicals in the
West End and throughout the world. Former pupils include: Jack
P. Shepherd, Kimberly Walsh, Emma Williams and Christian
Cooke. In December 2009 Valerie was awarded an MBE in the
Queen's New Years' Honours List, for services to the arts in the
north of England.

Megan Wheldon – Agent, Lou Coulson Associates
*I started in theatre working in wardrobe and then I moved to
Narrow Road, working for Tim Brown and Richard Ireson, and
then I heard from an actress I knew that someone was leaving
Lou's and had a curry with Lou and became an assistant. I've been
here 21 years, with three maternity breaks.*

PRODUCERS

Robert Banks Stewart – Independent TV producer/writer
(Darling Buds of May, Shoestring, Bergerac)
*I went into the army when I was 18 and worked in Field Marshal
Montgomery's Paris headquarters. Then I worked with* Illustrated
Magazine *as a magazine writer, travelling around the world – one
of the photographers I worked for was Ken Russell, when he was
a stills photographer. I had written a number of – a couple of stage*

plays.... I simply wanted to be a writer and I was very lucky because I knew what I wanted to do.

Tim Bradley – TV producer (Primeval, Silent Witness, Casualty)
I began carrying the cups of tea on a show called Lovejoy and progressed to moving the props around the room for other people for about three years, then location managed, then first assistant directed for about three years. And then I associated produced – which is kind of the smaller version of the proper external line producer.

John Griffin – Executive producer (Skins, Shameless, Wild at Heart, The Village, The White Queen)
I was 20 years an actor, mostly in theatre but also in television and radio, then became a script editor about ten years ago and from there became a producer and now executive producer for series at Company TV.

Alison Hindell – BBC Radio Drama Controller
I was a radio drama producer, then a senior drama producer in Wales, for about 15 years before I got this job. Before that I had been in the literary department of the RSC. So it was a theatre route, but I would say radio drama directors and producers – who are usually the same person by the way – are divided. Most people have a theatre background, but some do have a purely radio background, so their approach might differ from someone with a more theatrical, traditionally-trained background.

Diana Kyle – TV producer/executive producer (EastEnders, Silent Witness, Grange Hill, Holby City)
I was an actor for ten years, working consistently in theatre (touring and rep) along with some radio and TV. I joined the BBC Scenic Design and Visual Effects Department in London in 1984. I transferred to BBC Drama Production after two years, working my way up from Assistant Floor Manager, via Location Manager and Associate Producer to Producer. I produced several series including: Pig Heart Boy *(BAFTA winner);* Behind Closed Doors *(BAFTA nominee);* Wipeout *(BAFTA script winner);* Kidnapped *and a* Casualty/Holby *Special. I was Executive Producer in the BBC Children's Drama Department, developing and overseeing several projects (including* Bootleg, *BAFTA winner), before becoming Series Producer on* Holby City *(BAFTA winner).*

Simon Mirren – Producer/writer (Writer – for Casualty, Waking the Dead, producer/writer for Criminal Minds, Without a Trace, screen writer feature film for G:MT.)

I was 'on the tools', mixing plaster for a brand new kitchen. It was really posh and the builders asked me to ask the guy who owned the house what he did, how he got all his money. So I had to go and ask him, I knocked on his door and said, 'I'm sorry mate to disturb you but the boys want to know what you do because you clearly have a lot of money' and he said, 'I'm a writer' and I said, 'Oh, that's cool. What do you write?' And he said, 'Television shows, it's like a medical show', so I went down and said 'He writes TV...'

Marc Samuelson – Film producer (Honor, Ashes, Albatross, Me and Orson Welles, Alice Creed)

I did a Management Sciences degree at Manchester University… a very good degree for being a film producer because you end up getting a bit of an overview of law, accountancy, marketing, organizational psychology, industrial relations, financial institutions – which as a producer is fantastically useful. I then ran the trade association – the Association of Independent Producers, a forerunner of PACT, where I got to know a lot of people and then ran the Edinburgh TV festival. Then I worked for a producer called Simon Perry and we finished a film called 1984, which was from the George Orwell novel, and went on to make three more films, the biggest of which was White Mischief *directed by Michael Radford…. I was a baby producer – associate producer.*

James Schamus – Screenwriter/film producer
(Brokeback Mountain, Happiness, The Brothers McMullen)
James Schamus is an Academy Award–nominated screenwriter, producer, and film executive. His long collaboration as writer and producer for Ang Lee has resulted in 11 films, including *Brokeback Mountain*; *Crouching Tiger, Hidden Dragon*; *The Ice Storm*; *The Wedding Banquet*; *The Hulk*; *Taking Woodstock*, and *Lust, Caution*. He has also produced or executive-produced many of the most important American independent films of the past decade, including four Grand Prize winners at the Sundance Film Festival. He is a widely published film historian and theorist and Professor of Professional Practice in Columbia University's School of the Arts.

Beryl Vertue OBE – Independent television producer, executive producer, Hartswood Films
Beryl started out as a secretary, and became 'an agent by accident'. She looked after TV and radio writers Ray Galton, Alan Simpson,

Jonny Speight, Eric Sykes and Spike Milligan before joining the Stigwood Organization, specializing in selling British TV formats to America. She received the OBE in 2004, BAFTA awarded her the Alan Clarke Award for Outstanding Creative Contribution to Television, and on 20 March 2012 she was given a Lifetime Achievement Award at the Royal Television Society Programme Awards. Ten days later Beryl was presented with the Harvey Lee Award for Outstanding Contribution to Broadcasting at the Broadcasting Press Guild TV and Radio Awards.

Jo Ward – Executive producer, BBC (Grange Hill, Tracey Beaker Returns, Young Dracula)

I first entered the BBC as a temporary typist. I did a long apprenticeship in various departments and finally managed to get into television production and worked my way through all roles that then existed, which is fewer than there are now. I was finally line producing, looking after budgets, and a script passed my desk which I volunteered to produce because I loved it so much. I said, 'I will line produce it and produce it and save you money' and my boss at the time didn't let me do that but he did let me produce it. I had originally wanted to direct but decided that, actually, producing was more my style. I like to organize and manage and guide – that's what I think a Producer does.

Tim Welton – Theatre director/producer (freelance)

I trained at RADA as an actor and worked for about 15 years up and down the country. I worked with a small company called Wink – Rufus Norris, Natasha Chivers and Katrina Lindsay and I – but I didn't want to be a producer of a small company. In 2002 Rufus rang me up and said would I be his assistant at the Young Vic on Sleeping Beauty… *Rufus and I have this joke that we think we've worked together in every possible permutation in the theatre, you know: I've acted for him, he's acted for me in a show that I directed, we both sort of produced together – all of the permutations.*

DIRECTORS

J Blakeson – Film director

I made a couple of short films on 16mm at university and Nicky Lund, at that time a junior agent at David Higham Associates, saw one and told me to give her a call once I graduated. So I pestered her for about a year before she signed me up and I thought I was going to be a hugely famous film director by the time I was 22. Five years later I actually got a job as a screenwriter, and then I wrote for UK production companies like Working Title. Eventually I wrote a script that I planned to make myself, as I had experiences with previous scripts where they had been attached to a director and it had been very close but then never got made. I wanted to direct something, so I wrote a film called The Disappearance of Alice Creed *with the intention of making it myself – luckily somebody came in and financed it and made it with me, so I didn't have to make it on credit cards.*

Marina Caldarone – Theatre/radio director and author
(Actions: The Actors' Thesaurus and Radioactive monologues for Women/Men: for radio, stage and screen)
I did a drama degree and then was Howard Brenton's assistant on Bloody Poetry. *I worked on the Fringe in London, in Hong Kong and Italy and lots of student festivals and I learned more about how to direct than I had in three years at Uni. Then I won the RTYDS, which is now the Channel 4 Young Directors Award. I was Associate Director Theatr Clwyd and directed lots of Number 1 tours. I went to the National Theatre studio, then became Artistic Director of the Queens Theatre. I also do acting coaching in television and lecture on theatre.*

Damien Goodwin – Actor/film/theatre director and film, theatre, videogames/actor (Hollyoaks, Teachers, Jonathan Creek)
I trained at Central School of Speech and Drama and worked as an actor for about 14 years. I spent a lot of time when I was working as an actor in TV just sort of hanging out on the sets and picking up basics. I did a short course in a film school in order to brush up on the technical aspects of film and television. I started directing short films and then went to direct Hollyoaks, *for about three years. Then I moved into doing both the voice-over and performance capture direction on video games, working in dramality TV and a lot of development for TV and film.*

Mike Leigh – Film/theatre director and writer
Mike studied theatre at RADA and then studied further at Camberwell School of Art and the Central School of Art and Design. He began as a theatre playwright and director in the mid-1960s. His well-known films include *Life is Sweet, Topsy Turvy, Vera Drake* and *Happy-Go-Lucky,* in theatre his work includes the classic *Abigail's Party,* and more recently *Grief,* written and directed for the National Theatre.

Tim Schwab – Documentary filmmaker
Tim is Associate Professor at Concordia University in Montreal, Canada in the Department of Communication Studies. His documentary film *Being Osama* required the subjects to all have the name 'Osama' – an unusual casting requirement! He is currently

working on the Palestinian Filmmaker Project, featuring interviews and excerpts from the work of Palestinian filmmakers living throughout the Middle East.

Joe Sumsion – (Artistic Director, Dukes Theatre, Lancaster)

I was born and brought up in Kendal – 25 miles north of Lancaster. I got my Equity card here, at the Dukes, as an assistant stage manager when I was 19. I did a drama degree at Bristol University – but knew I wanted to direct. My first professional production was for Pocket Theatre, Cumbria, a touring theatre company, and then I got an Arts Council assistant director bursary at the Royal Theatre, Northampton. After that I worked as a freelance director and I was an associate director at the Theatre Royal, Stratford East – which was more about being a director of a theatre rather than directing plays. Before I came here I worked at Action Transport Theatre Company for seven years.

Pippa Harrison – Head of Client Relations, Spotlight

Pippa Harrison trained at Bretton Hall and Hull University. Pippa worked briefly as an actor as a founder member of Fecund Theatre then ran various small theatres and dance companies including The Tristan Bates Theatre, Union Dance Company and the International Theatre Forum. Pippa is currently Head of Client Relations at Spotlight.

■ APPENDICES

Useful information

SCRIPTS

When you send off your script to actors or agents, you must ensure that it is formatted correctly. If it isn't formatted professionally then it isn't professional. The industry standard programmes, which you will have to pay for are:

Final Draft: http://www.finaldraft.com/
Movie Magic: http://www.write-bros.com/

There is a free alternative:

CELTX: http://celtx.en.softonic.com/

which is adequate and will help you present in a professional manner.

Script Readings:
http://www.scriptfactory.co.uk/

In 1996 The Script Factory launched a season of screenplay readings by veteran screenwriters as a new art form celebrating the craft of writing for film. Steven Knight's *Dirty Pretty Things* was picked up after its Script Factory reading and the screenplay went on to Oscar nomination in 2002. *Lawless Heart*, written and directed by Neil Hunter and Tom Hunsinger and first aired on The Script Factory Stage, was premiered at the *Time Out* gala in the London Film Festival of 2001. Gavin Hood, whose filmmaking career spans *Tsotsi* as well as *X-Men Origins: Wolverine*, had his first script selected for a reading by The Script Factory, helping to raise his profile and launch his career.

The visceral reality of the readings brought the scripts to life and whilst this exposes the problems rather ruthlessly, it also demonstrates the production potential; as you sit back and close your eyes you are transported to the story world. Is it one you want to go to?

Lucy Scher – director, The Script Factory

SOURCING ACTORS

Spotlight
http://www.spotlight.com/

Over 40,000 performers appear in Spotlight, including actors and actresses, child artists, presenters, dancers and stunt artists.

Showcases (drama school, universities & colleges)
There will be a university, college course or drama school somewhere near you, where you can find talented students of all ages, abilities and ethnicities.

Drama Schools and training providers
http://www.dramauk.co.uk/

Drama UK, formed from the merger of the National Council for Drama Training (NCDT) and the Conference of Drama Schools (CDS), includes the accreditation of vocational courses and providing support to those organizations offering accredited training.

Their website enables you to search by location or by courses. Once you have found courses near to you, you can contact them.

Universities and Colleges
To find Dance, Drama and Performance courses at universities and colleges near you, go to www.ucas.com/students/coursesearch click on the red button saying 'search' type in 'drama' or 'performance' in the 'subject' box, 'all course types', 'all attendance types', 'all institutions', and finally choose the region you are interested in working in – you will be amazed at the number of courses that come up. Choose the ones you are interested in, click on 'about this institution' which will take you their web address. Find the appropriate course administrator or lecturer and email them with details of your production/casting needs.

Equity branches
http://www.equity.org.uk/

This can be an excellent place to make contact with actors in your area. Equity has a network of branches throughout the UK.

Members are invited to join their local branch and Equity student members are also very welcome at meetings. Some branches now have their own websites which include local news and directories of branch members, where you might be able to publicise your production.

TRADE AND INDUSTRY ORGANIZATIONS

BECTU
http://www.bectu.org.uk/

BECTU is the independent trade union for those working in broadcasting, film, theatre, entertainment, leisure, interactive media and allied areas. The union represents staff, contract and freelance workers who are based primarily in the United Kingdom.

Equity (UK)
http://www.equity.org.uk/

Equity Agreements are negotiated with employers and employer groups to cover all areas of live and recorded media. These collective agreements cover the detail of working terms and conditions such as numbers of performances, hours, breaks, health and safety, dispute procedures, usage rights, royalties, touring and a host of other things providing a coherent framework for a fast-moving industry.

Equity encourages emerging employers to work with them and has information for fringe companies and those making low budget films. If you are putting together a funding application make sure you include in the budget the correct Equity rates of pay for the artists. Check out the Equity rates or contact one of their helpdesks for more information.

Actors' Equity Association (USA)
http://www.actorsequity.org

This is the labour union that represents actors and stage managers in the United States. Equity negotiates wages and working conditions and provides a wide range of benefits, including health and pension plans, for its members. Actors' Equity is a member of the AFL-CIO, and is affiliated with FIA, an international organization of performing arts unions. Their website offers agreements for everything from Dinner Theatre to the Disneyworld Rulebook.

PACT
http://www.pact.co.uk/

PACT is the UK trade association representing and promoting the commercial interests of independent feature film, television, digital, children's and animation media companies. At the time of writing, the fee for Film Membership was £500 – plus an additional levy payment for each film registered with PACT – for a UK registered limited company that is producing feature films intended for theatrical release. You can choose to register just one film with PACT, which would still give you access to PACT/Equity contracts.

Independent Theatre Council (ITC)
http://www.itc-arts.org/

The Independent Theatre Council is the management association and industry body for performing arts organizations and individuals working in the field of drama, dance, opera and music theatre, mime and physical theatre, circus, puppetry, street arts and mixed media. ITC members are based throughout the UK and work extensively both nationally and across the world, producing some of the best new work in the performing arts today.

The Society of London Theatre
http://www.solt.co.uk

Founded in 1908 by Sir Charles Wyndham, the Society of London Theatre (SOLT) is the trade association that represents the producers, theatre owners and managers of the major commercial and grant-aided theatres in central London. Today the Society combines its long-standing roles in such areas as industrial relations and legal advice for members with a campaigning role for the industry, together with a wide range of audience-development programmes to promote theatre-going.

The Theatrical Management Association (TMA)
http://www.tmauk.org

Established in 1894, the TMA is a leading trade association representing the interests of, and providing professional support for, the performing arts in the UK. Members include theatres, multi-purpose venues, arts centres, concert halls, commercial producers, touring theatre, opera and ballet companies, sole traders and suppliers to the performing arts.

The Producers' Forum
http://www.producersforum.org.uk/

A membership based, sector-led professional organization providing training, networking, and a cohesive lobbying voice for independent filmmakers in the creative sector.

SAG-AFTRA (Screen Actors Guild and the American Federation of Television and Radio Artists)
http://www.sag.org

Represents actors, announcers, broadcast journalists, dancers, DJ's, news writers, news directors, program hosts, puppeteers, recording artists, singers, stunt performers, voiceover artists and other media professionals. Their website offers contract samples and signatory packages for everything from student films, short films and ultra-low budget films through to feature films for theatrical release.

SAG-AFTRA is committed to organizing all work done under their jurisdictions; negotiating the best wages, working conditions, and health and pension benefits; preserving and expanding members' work opportunities; vigorously enforcing their contracts; and protecting members against unauthorized use of their work. SAG-AFTRA partners with fellow unions internationally to seek the strongest protections for media artists throughout the world.

The Casting Directors' Guild
http://www.thecdg.co.uk/

The Guild is a professional organisation of casting directors in the film, television, theatre and commercials communities in the UK and Ireland who have joined together to further their common interests in establishing a recognized standard of professionalism in the industry, enhancing the stature of the profession, providing a free exchange of information and ideas, honouring the achievements of members and standardization of working practices within the industry.

PUBLICATIONS

CONTACTS: *Stage, Television, Film and Radio*
http://www.spotlight.com/shop/contacts.

Every year, Spotlight, publishes a new edition of *Contacts*. This directory contains over 5000 listings for companies, services and individuals across all branches of television, stage, film and radio. Information is updated annually to provide the most accurate information available.

AUDITION VENUES

CONTACTS has a comprehensive list of spaces for hire for rehearsals, auditions and interviews. You can also look on-line for local church halls, rooms above pubs, community centres etc.

CONTRACTS

If at all possible you should aim to use an industry standard contract. Even if you have no budget, it is still worthwhile familiarizing yourself with the contracts that you will be using in the future as a guide to best practice.

Without a budget, you must still adhere to industry standard, negotiated working hours and breaks.

CHILDREN

Performance licences are subject to legislation – The Children's Performance Regulations 1968. Make sure you go to the appropriate licensing authority – that is, where the child *lives* not where they go to school.

This site will direct you to the appropriate local authority address where you need to apply for the child license:
http://local.direct.gov.uk/LDGRedirect/index.jsp?LGSL=48&LGIL=8

There is an interesting interview (US based but informative for UK also) on working with and employing child actors here:
http://www.videojug.com/interview/child-casting-basics-4

Children's agencies

You will find a comprehensive list of children's agents in CONTACTS.

Below is a selection. It is also worth researching locally for youth groups, drama classes and clubs.

Sylvia Young Theatre School – based in London.
http://www.sylviayoungtheatreschool.co.uk/

Ravenscourt Theatre School – West London. Tel: 020 8741 0707

Mark Jermin Stage School – various locations in Wales and London.
http://www.markjermin.co.uk/

Stage 84 – based in Bradford.
http://www.stage84.com/

The Television Workshop – Nottingham.
http://www.thetelevisionworkshop.co.uk

Stagecoach – a nationwide, franchised, organization which runs weekly classes for children up to 18, http://www.stagecoach.co.uk

A & J Management – North London.
http://www.ajmanagement.co.uk

Children's working hours are dependent on age.
The rules apply to children under 17. From the summer of 2013, a young person must do some part-time education or training until they're 17, so licensing and employment permits will apply until they are 18.

Above this age they are considered to be adults by law, and must be treated as such. The hours a child or young person can work differ depending on whether it is term time or holidays – always check for up-to-date legislation. See: https://www.gov.uk/child-employment/minimum-ages-children-can-work

There are restrictions on call times and lengths of 'continuous performance'. The maximum hours a day a child can work includes travelling time to and from set/location.

SOME USEFUL WEBSITES:
https://www.nowcasting.com/indexsplash.html
http://www.starnow.co.uk/
http://www.talentcircle.org/
http://shootingpeople.org/home
http://www.backstage.com/bso/index.jsp
http://www.pcrnewsletter.com/pcr/
http://www.thestage.co.uk/recruitment/
http://www.castingcallpro.com/uk/
http://www.whorepresents.com/

Casting Call Pro
A well-respected website for advertising jobs and networking contacts.
http://www.castingcallpro.com/uk

Mandy
For young producers, actors and directors for short and student films.
http://www.mandy.com

Arts Jobs – the Arts Council free mailing list service
http://www.artsjobs.org.uk

LEGAL
The BBC has a useful website which gives guidance on casting and the legalities.
http://www.bbc.co.uk/filmnetwork/filmmaking/guide/production/cast-and-crew#cast

Shooting People, the independent filmmaking community, has a resources section on their website with downloadable contracts and release forms. Contracts include: paid cast and crew contracts; unpaid collaboration contracts and documentary, location, footage and photography release forms. NB You need to be a paid-up member to access these resources.
http://shootingpeople.org/resources.php

Another useful site (US based) for release forms for different artists' contributions is:
http://www.videouniversity.com/articles/releases-for-use-in-film-and-video/

Volunteers and the Law by Mark Restall – for a free downloadable version go to:
http://www.volunteering.org.uk/publications

Volunteering England is the national volunteering development organization for England. It provides support systems to assist anyone involved with volunteers.

VOLUNTEER AGREEMENT

Thank you for offering your assistance in supporting XXXXXXX - as a Volunteer

This is an agreement to set out the relationship between XXXXX and anyone seeking the opportunity to be a Volunteer and gain some experience of XXXXX. This record is therefore not a binding contract - nor an offer or a basis of work- or employment now or in the future.

This form is to be completed and signed by the Volunteer prior to starting the activities, counter signed at the same time by the relevant delegated person, and copies retained by both the volunteer and the Production office.

Whilst involved in any agreed activities, a Volunteer is covered by the production insurance as appropriate.

A Volunteer's reasonable personal expenses as incurred will be reimbursed.

Volunteer Surname.../First Name...

Address..

Mobile../Email..

Volunteer Role...

Project Title/Activity..

Dates: from............./................./.............../to........../............./........../Total days...................................

To be briefed by..

Reporting to..

Nationality.. /Fluent spoken and written English   Y / N

Clean Driving Licence   Y / N   First Aid/ Health & Safety training..

Health: Will you require any adjustments or provisions to be made?..

Emergency contact person...

Relationship.../Phone..

Competency / Experience for the role../CV attached   Y / N

By accepting this position of Volunteer on XXXXX I understand and accept that no matter what my role or possible creative contribution to a project, I have no basis for any subsequent claim to any copyright established by such activities and that in the event of there being any such rights created, I acknowledge that they reside entirely within the sole control of XXXX.

I confirm that the information I have given here is correct – and that and this completed form and my CV may be held on file by XXXXX - as evidence of my being an 'approved volunteer' in the event of my wishing to be considered for another opportunity in the future.

Volunteer (Signed).../Date.........../.................../...............

For the production
(Signed).../Date.............../...................../...............

Address of Company   Company no.   Tel: URL

■ GLOSSARY

Action
The descriptions or stage directions in a script, i.e. not dialogue

ADR
Additional dialogue recording – is the process of re-recording original dialogue after filming is completed.

Agent
The actor's representative.

Attached
An actor who has agreed, in principle, to be part of a project.

Available/availability
Whether an artist is free to work on specific dates for filming, rehearsals and/or performances.

Be put up (for a part)
An actor is suggested for, or suggests themselves, for a role.

Beat
The internal rhythm of a speech or line.

Big (as in a performance that is too big)
The screen can magnify every expression, potentially making a performance appear unbelievable.

Block (of episodes)
More than one episode, but less than an entire series.

Breakdown
Description of character/s and production details.

Budget
The financial plan for a project, or specific area of a project.

Call sheets
Daily, detailed schedule of production including actors' working hours.

Casting advice note
Information and contact sheet including any financial agreement.

Casting director
Responsible for finding actors.

Cold
Asking an actor to read with no preparation.

CONTACTS
Published by Spotlight – contains listings for over 5000 companies, services and individuals across all branches of TV, stage, film and radio.

Cross-casting
Within a company, actors are cast to play different roles, in two or more plays, that are staged alternately and regularly over several weeks or months.

CV/resume
A list of an actor's credits and skills.

Deal memo
See 'casting advice note'.

Devised
A performance that has been created without having a completed script.

Ensemble
A script where there is no specific 'lead' character but instead there is a group of characters, all of whom develop and share the narrative.

Expenses
Costs incurred by the actor in order to work on a project.

Eye in (as in 'getting your eye in')
Allowing time to get a sense of the type of actors you like and feel are right for your project.

Feel
The tempo, energy and timbre of the piece.

For hire
Any professional who is employed to work on a project, as opposed to instigating and developing it.

Go up
An actor being suggested for or suggesting themselves for a role.

Head of department (HOD)
In charge of an area of production.

Headshot
Professionally taken photograph of an actor.

Hot (as in 'this actor will pull an audience because they are currently very popular')
An actor who has a current high profile and would bring attention and finance to a project.

IMDB (International Movie DataBase)
Online database of information relating to film, tv, actors and crew.

IMDB Pro (subscription required)
As above, but has more in-depth information, such as actors' managers, agents, and further contact details for individuals and companies.

Improvisation
Spontaneously reacting to stimuli that may or may not be script based.

In-house
A casting person or department that is employed full time by a company.

Lead/s
The pivotal character/s in a script.

Locked
Confirmed shooting dates.

Marquee value
A name that when advertised on billboards will have the power to attract an audience.

Name (as in 'a name')
An actor with profile and track record of well-known acting work and/or an actress/actor/performer/celebrity whose profile will bring finance and publicity.

Number 1 tour
A touring theatre production which goes to major theatres in large cities nationally.

An actor means something...
Do they mean something to the sales agent or distribution, i.e will they attract audience and money?

Off –book
An actor having learned their lines and no longer needing a script in hand.

Offer
Terms that are proposed to an actor or their agent regarding a specific job.

On board
Anyone who has agreed terms and is committed to a project.

On tape
To tape or record an actor reading a scene for a part.

Pages
Selection of scenes from a script sent to actors prior to a meeting.

Period piece
A script that is not set in the present day.

Playing range (actor)
The ages at which the actor can be believably cast.

Quality
The adjectives used to describe the emotional and non-visual aspects of a character or performer.

Reading
Hearing a scene or a script out loud.

Reading in
Someone reading the other roles whilst an actor is auditioning.

Recall
Asking an actor to a further meeting to audition and/or read for the same role

Regular characters
Characters that recur in a series or serial.

Repertory
A permanent company that produces regular work.

Research
Investigating the background and context of a script and its characters.

SAG-AFTRA
Screen Actors' Guild and American Federation of TV and Radio Artists (USA) – Actors' Union that has agreements in place for actors working in all recorded media.

Showcase
Presentation by a group of performers of short scenes or speeches.

Showreel
Selections of an actors' on-screen work, edited together.

Sides
See 'Pages' above.

Spotlight
A UK directory of actors and actresses.

Star
An actor whose name is instantly recognizable to an audience.

Street Casting
Looking in non-professional environments for non-actors.

Stunt Casting
Approaching a high profile individual to appear in your project.

Synopsis
A brief outline of the plot and characters.

Taste
Personal likes and dislikes.

Theatre in Education (TIE)
Usually touring theatre, with an educational aspect and agenda.

Through-cast
An actor cast in a variety of roles in a season of plays.

Type
A way of defining the characteristics of a role.

Typecast
To typecast is to cast an actor in a role that is similar, or the same, as one that they are known for playing or have played before.

Workshop audition
Designed for a group of actors or performers rather than seeing them individually.

EXERCISES

■ **Exercise 1**

Get each member of your creative team to fill in the empty boxes with the names of actors they think express the qualities described.

QUALITIES	ACTOR
Warmth, humour, empathy	
Energy, intensity	
Sexuality, vulnerability	
Physicality, cheekiness	
Warmth, intelligence	
Sexuality, humour?	

Compare the names of the actors you have come up with – discuss the actors named and where you agree and disagree.

■ **Exercise 2**

This exercise will help articulate your taste.

FAVOURITE ACTORS	REASONS

FAVOURITE ACTRESSES	REASONS

To help you identify the qualities different actors can bring to a film production, name your favourite actor or actress from different genres.

GENRE	ACTOR	REASONS
Action		
Costume/historical		
Fantasy		
Animation		
Thriller		
Musical		
Zombie		
Horror		

To help you identify the qualities different actors can bring to a theatre production, name your favourite actor or actress who you have seen perform in the following.

GENRE	ACTOR	REASONS
Classical		
New writing		
Comedy		
Contemporary		
Shakespeare		
Musical		
Site Specific		
Pantomime		
Stand up		

■ **Exercise 4 – knowing your taste**

Think of six actors: three women and three men, with an assortment of ages and nationalities.

What is it you like about them? What qualities do they have?

GENDER	AGE	NATIONALITY	ACTOR	WHAT DO YOU LIKE ABOUT THEM	DEFINING QUALITIES
Male	17 – 25	British			
Female	17 – 25	British			
Male	60+	North American			
Female	60+	North American			
Male	35 – 40	European			
Female	35 – 40	European			

TEMPLATES

■ Dissect your script

Each member of your team should complete their own chart then compare before deciding who to see.

CHARACTER	GENDER	AGE	NATIONALITY/ ETHNICITY	ACTOR	WHAT DO YOU LIKE ABOUT THEM	DEFINING QUALITIES

■ Developing your breakdown

CHARACTER	DATES	SPECIAL REQUIREMENTS	PLAYING AGE	GENDER	ETHNICITY	DESCRIPTION

CASTING BREAKDOWN

TITLE:

COMPANY:

DATES OF REHEARSAL:

DATES OF PERFORMANCES:

LOCATION OF REHEARSALS:

LOCATION OF PERFORMANCES:

FEE OR EXPENSES:

NAME OF DIRECTOR:

SYNOPSIS:

CHARACTERS TO BE CAST:

CONTACT DETAILS:
email:
phone:
fax:

DEADLINE DATE FOR CASTING SUBMISSIONS:

DATES OF CASTING/WORKSHOPS:

A CHECKLIST FOR MEETING WITH THE ARTIST

Send out clear directions for the meeting – including a Google reference if appropriate.	
Give the agent your contact number.	
Have a contact number for the actor's agent with you.	
Have a copy of the script with you and any other details you might need – e.g. mood board or synopsis/ideas.	
Get to the meeting place half an hour ahead of time to secure a table and make sure it is not too noisy for your meeting, especially if the meeting is in a public cafe.	
Have enough money with you to pay for a beverage for the actor and yourselves.	
Set a time limit for the meeting – an hour maximum.	
Have a list of questions prepared to ask/get the conversation going.	

■ Deciding who to see

CHARACTER	ACTOR NAME	CONTACT INFORMATION	REASONS FOR SEEING

Meeting organization

NAME	BEING SEEN FOR	AGENT/CONTACT DETAILS	AVAILABILITY	MEETING DATE/ TIME	PAGES SENT

Who does what at the audition

TASK	NAME	PREPARE
Meet and greet		
Lead the meeting		
Talk about the project		
Talk about the CV		
Read in with the actor		
Camera operation		

Audition Timings

TITLE OF PROJECT:

VENUE OF CASTING SESSION:

DATE/TIME OF CASTING SESSION:

NAMES OF DIRECTOR/PRODUCER:

CONTACT NUMBERS:

Team to meet in: (*insert venue*) at (*insert time*)

Room and camera set up: (*insert time*)

TIME*	NAME	ROLE	AGENT/CONTACT
	Re-cap/discussion		
	Session finishes		

PRE-CASTING SESSION CHECKLIST – MAKE SURE YOU HAVE CHECKED ALL THESE BOXES.

TO DO	CHECK
Put notices on the doors with clear arrows directing actors where to go.	
Try to position the waiting area out of earshot of the audition.	
Lay out printed information about your production or company for actors to read.	
Arrange tables and chairs for the team who will be in the room.	
Ensure the actor will be able to make eye contact with everyone from their chair.	
Clear away extra tables and chairs if you are running a workshop audition.	
Organize CVs of all the actors you are going to see and ensure all those in the session have a copy.	
Ensure everyone in the room has something to make notes on.	
Test the camera – ensure the sound is working – and check framing.	
Have spare copies of the pages/script so that everyone in the room has a copy and ensure there are enough spares for actors if they have forgotten theirs.	
Ensure meeter and greeter has a phone and the numbers of the actors and agents.	
Ensure everyone in the session has a copy of the timings sheet.	

Post Audition Feedback Form

	ACTOR'S NAME/ SEEN FOR	ACTOR'S NAME	ACTOR'S NAME	ACTOR'S NAME	ACTOR'S NAME	ACTOR'S NAME	ACTOR'S NAME	ACTOR'S NAME
Initial thoughts *Were they what you expected in look or feel?*								
Reaction to reading *Was it what you expected?* *Did it surprise you?* *Were you excited/interested?* *Did you like their choices?*								
Qualities of actor *Your impression – does he/she match with your vision of the role?*								
Second reading *Did they carry out direction/notes?* *What effect did it have on their reading/the character?* *Was it better/worse/the same?*								
Overall *Could you work with them creatively?* *Did you like their thoughts on the project/ character?* *Would they work with the other actors you have in mind or have cast?*								
Could you see actor as the character?								
Recall or offer or 'no'?								

(Title of project)

CASTING ADVICE NOTE

(Date)   *(Number of casting advice note)*

Name: *(name of actor)*

Part: *(name of role)*

Address:

Tel:

Email:

Agent: *(if actor has an agent)*

Tel:

Email:

Fee: *(or expenses only/travel/profit share)*

Dates:

Any other stipulations agreed:

Timeline for casting children

Remember to start your research no less than three months before your scheduled start of production.

Script lock/ character breakdowns	Research and discussion	Children's workshops/ auditions	Recall workshops/ decision	Licensing paperwork	Licence granted/ production begins

Checklist for child license

Make sure you go to the appropriate licensing authority – that is, where the child *lives* not where they go to school.

Item	Check
Details and signature of parent	
Medical questionnaire completed and signed by parent	
Photographs of child (2 × identical photographs)	
Medical Certificate/Doctor's letter	
Original Birth Certificate	
Headteacher's permission	

VOLUNTEER AGREEMENT

Thank you for offering your assistance in supporting   - as a Volunteer

This is an agreement to set out the relationship between   and anyone seeking the opportunity to be a Volunteer and gain some experience of   . This record is therefore not a binding contract - nor an offer or a basis of work- or employment now or in the future.

This form is to be completed and signed by the Volunteer prior to starting the activities, counter signed at the same time by the relevant delegated person, and copies retained by both the volunteer and the Production office.

Whilst involved in any agreed activities, a Volunteer is covered by the production insurance as appropriate.

A Volunteer's reasonable personal expenses as incurred will be reimbursed.

Volunteer Surname.../First Name...

Address..

Mobile.../Email..

Volunteer Role...

Project Title/Activity...

Dates: from.............../.................../.............../to.........../.............../.........../Total days...

To be briefed by...

Reporting to...

Nationality... /Fluent spoken and written English   Y / N

Clean Driving Licence   Y / N   First Aid/ Health & Safety training...

Health: Will you require any adjustments or provisions to be made?...

Emergency contact person..

Relationship../Phone..

Competency / Experience for the role.../CV attached   Y / N

By accepting this position of Volunteer on   I understand and accept that no matter what my role or possible creative contribution to a project, I have no basis for any subsequent claim to any copyright established by such activities and that in the event of there being any such rights created, I acknowledge that they reside entirely within the sole control of   .

I confirm that the information I have given here is correct – and that and this completed form and my CV may be held   on file by   - as evidence of my being an 'approved volunteer' in the event of my wishing to be considered for another opportunity in the future.

Volunteer (Signed).../Date............/.................../...............

For the production
(Signed).../Date.............../...................../...............

■ INDEX

A page reference in bold indicates a glossary term.